MARK D TUBBS

BLUEPRINT FOR YOUR DESTINY

A Step-by-Step Guide

BLUEPRINT FOR YOUR DESTINY: A STEP-BY-STEP GUIDE

By Dr. Mark D Tubbs

®Copyright 2024-Mark Tubbs

All rights reserved. This book is protected by the copyright laws of the United States of America. This book may not be copied or reprinted for commercial gain or profit. The use of short quotations is permitted.

Scripture quotations are from The Passion Translation, ® Copyright by Broadstreet Publishing. Used by permission, all rights reserved.

CONTENTS

FOREWORD BY DR. BRIAN SIMMONS 5

NOTES FROM THE EDITOR: "AN ENGINEERS PERSPECTIVE" 9

PREFACE 11

ACKNOWLEDGEMENTS 14

CHAPTER 1 | The Five Toes of God: Walking Out the Fivefold Ministry.. 17

CHAPTER 2 | The Steps to Reading a Blueprint 23

CHAPTER 3 | What is My Blueprint? 29
    Step 1: Read the Title Block (*the Author & Project*)

CHAPTER 4 | The Destiny Equation 44
    Step 2: Read the Revision Block (*Changes as you Mature*)

CHAPTER 5 | The Word as Our Guide 51
    Step 3: Read the Notes & Legends (*The Word as the Foundation*)

CHAPTER 6 | Seeing Through the Eyes of God and Others 83
    Step 4: Determine the View (*God's View, Others, and Shared*)

CHAPTER 7 | How to Measure Your Sphere of Authority 97
    Step 5: Establish the Scale (*Measuring Your Assigned Spheres*)

CHAPTER 8 | Where is My Ministry?..123
    Step 6: Inspect the Grid System (*Where do you Belong?*)

CHAPTER 9 | From Design into Destiny 130
    Step 7: Finish Schedule (*Write a "Destiny Declaration"*)

ADDITIONAL RESOURCES 148

FOREWORD BY DR. BRIAN SIMMONS

Everyone has a destiny! In our journey through life, we often find ourselves searching for meaning and purpose. We yearn to know why we are here, and what our unique role is in the grand tapestry of existence. It is within this quest for significance that we encounter the timeless truth that each one of us is designed with a purpose in mind. We are not mere accidents of fate, but rather intricately woven beings, created by a loving God who has crafted a blueprint for our destiny.

In "Blueprint for Your Destiny" Mark Tubbs leads us on a transformative exploration of how to walk out our divine callings. Like reading a blueprint, we discover that there are seven methods we can employ to identify and clarify our unique purpose. This book serves as a guiding light, illuminating the path toward understanding and embracing God's design for our lives.

At the core of this book lies the profound understanding that we are not passive bystanders in our destinies. Rather, we are active participants, called to build upon our understanding of the Fivefold ministry and apply it practically to our lives. Drawing upon the analogy of a blueprint, the author skillfully demonstrates how we can navigate the intricate details of our calling, step by step, ensuring that we align our lives with God's divine plan.

Throughout the pages of this book, we are reminded of the reality of God, our Creator and destiny designer. We are invited to explore the depths of His wisdom and the beauty of His intricate craftsmanship. As we dive into the material, we will uncover the passions and burdens that the Holy Spirit has lovingly placed upon our hearts. We will learn how to grow and mature, making intentional changes that will focus and guide us toward fulfilling our purpose.

Central to this journey is the understanding that the Scriptures are our compass, leading us into the fundamental truths and nurturing relationships necessary to walk into the fullness of our calling. As we delve into the Word of God, we discover a wealth of wisdom and guidance that will equip us to live out our divine destinies. This book serves as a faithful companion, guiding us through the sacred text and helping us apply its timeless teachings to our everyday lives.

One of the most valuable aspects of "Blueprint for Your Destiny" is the revelation of the three views of God's blueprint for our lives. The Plan view allows us to see the broader perspective, gaining insight into the grand purpose that encompasses our existence. The Elevation view provides us with a heightened understanding of the unique gifts and talents we possess, offering a clear picture of how we can use them for God's glory. Finally, the Sectional view allows us to examine the intricate details, revealing the steps we must take to fulfill our calling.

In our pursuit of destiny, it is crucial that we recognize and embrace our realms of influence and authority. This book empowers us to identify the areas where we can make a lasting impact, allowing us to walk confidently in the authority bestowed upon us by God. As we uncover the depths of our purpose, we will discover that our lives are not limited to the confines of the everyday; rather, they have the potential to shape history and transform the world around us.

I have been a friend to Mark Tubbs for many years and I've seen countless times his wisdom and expertise in helping others find their calling. Mark will be a fantastic tour guide for you in your journey into divine destiny. His experience both nationally and internationally in shifting cultures and mindsets is noteworthy. This book will not disappoint you but rather delight you in discovering your unique design and calling.

As you embark on this journey through "Blueprint for Your Destiny," I encourage you to approach it with an open heart and a willing spirit. Allow the words on these pages to penetrate deep into your soul, and may you be inspired to embrace the unique plan that God has intricately designed for you. May this book serve as a roadmap, guiding you through the seven steps to reading God's blueprint for your life. May it empower you to step into the fullness of your calling.

DR. BRIAN SIMMONS

Passion and Fire Ministries
The Passion Translation

NOTES FROM THE EDITOR:
"AN ENGINEER'S PERSPECTIVE"

As a retired mechanical engineer with more than 35 years experience in the design of high-tech military hardware, I jumped at the opportunity of editing this unique book. In my career, my job duties were all about producing blueprints and interpreting MIL-SPECS. With an accurate set of graphic documentation, anything can be produced.

The following is what makes this book so unusual. It's a collection of analogies comparing Christian teachings to the various and many components of an engineering blueprint. So cleverly conceived, but there's much more. It's a workbook which, if followed correctly, will be a lifetime treasure with lots of notes and entries in the places provided. It asks challenging questions. In addition, the author gives intimate and personal experiences to help motivate the reader to grow as a believer despite the circumstances. It was a pleasure to give my input to this project and surely it was inspired by the Holy Spirit.

JOHN KENNELLY
Editor of Blueprint for Your Destiny

PREFACE

One of the main questions I received as a pastor from congregants was, "What is my destiny?" Regardless of age everyone has a desire to know their created purpose. For ten years as a local pastor my focus had little to do with that question. I learned in seminary to build a growing church and there were even formulas to do that. In fact, there was not one class in three years that emphasized the role of equipping and what that may look like.

After ten years of full-time pastoring the earth shook and our whole paradigm shifted. What caused this to happen? In essence, Ann and I encountered God in a deep and profound way by learning to hear His voice. Even though Jesus stated that reality in John 10, "My sheep hear my voice", we never were mentored or even encouraged to do this.

This ability to hear God in a personal way began in 1996. As I personally began to hear God's voice in a practical way, that is through listening and journaling, the message from Him was consistent. For months all I heard was how much the Lord loves me. Repeatedly, with real and powerful encounters, the love of God was poured into my heart. I heard the Lord tell me that He created me, chose me, loved me, and set me apart. He told me I belonged to Him, and that He belonged to me. These experiences were matched with deep and profound feelings that I had never experienced before. My focus went from just head knowledge to an encounter in my heart.

We also focused on testing the words and confirming with the Scriptures. We did not want to be in error, and know the written Word is the standard to measure all we proport to hear. As I matured and sought the Lord, I began to hear words about my destiny and purpose. This book shares this journey with you utilizing the analogy of a blueprint. I believe our journeys are not just a linear experience, they are more like a winding road up and down the mountains. Yet, this analogy can help us follow the main direction of our lives.

The process may have been a journey, but early in this pursuit my purpose started to become very clear to me. This happened through a growing understanding of my primary and secondary Fivefold gifts, along with a focus on my passion and burden. This is all explained in a later chapter. Yet, I need to say it here that my purpose is to help people discover their destiny. During the shift in our ministry in 1996, we started to see the value in each person and the call upon all of our lives. This brought a whole new understanding of what equipping really is. To train me in what I was hearing, the Spirit led me to Kenya where I brought teams on an annual basis starting in 1999. It was there I saw people go from "pew sitters" to "freedom fighters." Sometimes this would happen in a matter of days.

Nothing excites me more than seeing people get released into greater freedom and getting glimpses of what how they would appear in maturity. In 2006 I wrote my first book "The Five Fingers of God: Discovering Your Destiny Through the Fivefold." To the glory of God this book has

PREFACE

been translated into 13 languages and been taught all over the world. We have also conducted services and training in over 40 nations.

In essence this book is a collection of the teachings that have developed because of focusing on the topic of destiny. Along the way, I would teach, "The Fivefold is not the building, it is like a blueprint. God has designed you perfectly and He wants to reveal what your calling is." There you have it, the motivation and articulation of why I have written "Blueprint For Your Destiny." It is my hope that it can become a valuable tool for anyone that wants to know their destiny in a clearer way. More than that, how to put this understanding into practice.

ACKNOWLEDGEMENTS

It is a joy to start with acknowledging my Lord and Savior. He is the author and perfector of my faith. I feel so loved and nurtured by God in this entire process of discovering my destiny. When I received Jesus Christ into my heart in 1978, I knew that it was going to become the foundation of my life. As I was about to graduate from college in 1981, my goal was to become a lawyer. Right before graduation I felt a tangible call to full time pastoral ministry. Along this journey, the Lord has opened many doors to over 40 nations, and the primary focus has been assisting people in discovering their destiny through the Fivefold ministry. In other words, all that I share in this book is from my personal experience. It is not based on theory, but in the perspective of a practitioner.

This is my third book, and the acknowledgements appear to be very much like the last two. Rightly so, my wife Ann is an inspiration to me. Her pursuit of God and commitment to teach others how to be close to Him has impacted everyone around her, especially me! She is the main reason we experienced a shift from powerless religion into world shaking relationship with Him. She always wants more of His presence and equips others to experience this in the most practical and personal ways.

Our apostles, Dr. Che and Sue Ahn, believe in us and have been a continuing encouragement to recognize what the Father is doing in and through our lives. Even though

ACKNOWLEDGEMENTS

our roles have transitioned over the years, the partnership and opening of doors has been consistent.

Along the way the past decade, Dr. Brian and Candice Simmons have been great friends, examples, and mentors in our lives. They model how to treat everyone with value while they pursue their destiny with fierce dedication. We love them with all our hearts and enjoy the partnership we share not only in friendship but in providing opportunities for fun and fellowship on trips to Israel, cruises, and trips to Cabo San Lucas.

Starting in 2018, we started a small relational network called "TRANSFORMATION OF THE NATIONS." The network is essentially made up of those who are called to align with us as apostles, spiritual parents, mentors, or partners. We are so grateful to this family that invites us to do real hands-on apostolic work. As a result, we are welcomed as family members into numerous congregations and ministries. Many of these are local church leaders, but recently the Spirit has been leading world-changing marketplace ministers to us.

We are so grateful to our spiritual son and daughter in Kenya for over 25 years. Apostle Simon and Selena are so dear to us, and we have raised them up into their ministry in East Africa. By God's amazing grace we have over 7000 churches in our network which is a part of the HIM global family. As indigenous leaders, they have created a movement where people are called into the fullness of Christ and maturity.

There are many people we could or should mention by name. We are grateful for our natural children and those who call us "Papa" and "Mama." We don't ask or tell anyone to do this, but voluntarily they do it in a way of honor and declaring that God is using us in their lives in a special way. The truth is, we are the ones that receive blessings and love. What a privilege.

In the process of preparing this book, my stepfather John Kennelly is my editor. He has spent endless hours poring over my books, and I am so grateful. My daughter Loraina does the final review, she prepares the book for printing, and does the design of the cover and other touches. She also has other intangible inputs that help me finalize crucial details of the presentation. One time she flatly rejected my book title and helped me choose a new one (hers!).

Lastly, I want to thank the people that have affirmed and appreciated the books. Also, to the many that trusted me in their church or ministry to train and equip the people entrusted to them as leaders. It is a joy to have people that believe in your message and offer encouragement over and over again.

CHAPTER 1

THE FIVE TOES OF GOD: WALKING OUT THE FIVEFOLD MINISTRY

It is crazy to think it was 19 years ago that I wrote my first book, *"The Five Fingers of God."* It was in the Fall of 2005 when I wrote my PhD thesis on the Fivefold ministry. At the time I was the Senior Pastor of Rock Creek Church in Portland, Oregon. The next year God launched me into a Global ministry through Harvest International Ministry. Until starting this book, I had no idea how significant my writing would be for my life. It was actually a declaration of my life and the call has gone from blueprint to fulfilling my destiny. In other words, I have been walking out what I wrote and foresaw in the book and much more.

During the past 19 years I have taught Fivefold ministry in almost every imaginable setting. As of now the Five Fingers of God has been translated into 13 languages. I have never initiated the translations personally; it has always been by the initiation of others. That means that it has met a need and assisted people in the goal of discovering their destiny.

This leads to the reason I have written this book. With years of experience as an apostle working full time with

Harvest International Ministry (2006-2018) and leading our own network for the past five years, my focus has been on how to bring individuals, ministries, and movements into the honor culture of the Fivefold ministry. In 2018 we started full time into our own network called, "Transformation of the Nations," to build a family of Fivefold leaders with the sole purpose of equipping leaders into their purpose and destiny.

Now is the time to glean from this amazing season and to add line upon line to what I wrote in 2005. Instead of revising, I believe it will be far more helpful to articulate how to identify, interpret, and implement the five-fold into your personal life and expression of this into all the spheres of culture. I also believe that a broader approach to discovering our destiny is important, and this book seeks to accomplish this goal.

THE FIVE TOES OF GOD

Ok, this is downright silly. If you have not read my first book, "The Five Fingers of God", you may have missed my attempt at humor. I was tempted to entitle this book, "The Five Toes of God." However, there was no other reason than to make a silly joke. Oh well, it was worth a chuckle. Regardless, there is a challenge in this humorous possible title, we must walk out practically what the Fivefold really is. It is one thing to talk about it, but where does it relate to your life practically?

Like other familiar topics, a lot of people say they believe in and understand the Fivefold ministry. However, when you talk about it with them or examine their life or ministry, you quickly discover it isn't a topic they have integrated practically into their lives. This is true about many topics in Scripture.

For me the Fivefold is an amazing method to release people into their destiny and purpose. When I encounter people, I quickly can see the Fivefold ministries that are motivating and driving them. By the leading of the Holy Spirit, I begin to see fundamental aspects of a person's purpose. To me, the Fivefold is not a fad, it is at the foundation of our creation and unfolds our purpose. The Fivefold ministries are like a blueprint.

THE FIVEFOLD AS A BLUEPRINT

The Fivefold is not the main goal, but a process. It is a tool, or in the context of this book, I am calling it a blueprint. To construct a building, you start with a design. The design is more than ideas and concepts. It is the product of meticulous planning and the expertise of an architect. In this analogy, God is the architect of our lives.

In Jeremiah 1:5 it says, "Before I formed you in the womb I knew you, before you were born I set you apart; I appointed you as a prophet to the nations." (NIV). This is a powerful personal verse. It speaks to God's forming us and setting us apart. The amazing truth is that this happens before we are even formed by His hand. God is our creator, and He knew you and me even before we were conceived. As our creator, He had a specific plan and call upon our life.

That is why I call the Fivefold a blueprint. It starts with God's design. Certainly, the blueprint contains far more than the Fivefold ministries. However, God told Jeremiah,

"I appointed you as a prophet to the nations." This is a specific assignment in the design of Jeremiah's life. When we accept and truly believe this is true for us, it can release a deep level of peace and joy when we contemplate our existence. We do have a purpose!

There are many other aspects to the blueprint that transcend the Fivefold ministry. As with any analogy, it breaks down at some point. The emphasis in these pages is not really our blueprint, but our relationship with God. Our identity comes from God and our purpose flows out of that. This book focuses on the purpose aspect of the blueprint, like the way that God spoke to Jeremiah.

BLUEPRINT FOR INVIDIVUALS AND MORE

I get very excited about talking and applying the Fivefold to an individual's life. When we look from a broader perspective, we can see that the Fivefold applies to virtually every area of our life. For example, I believe that God has a purpose for all of our relationships, as well as every organization that we may interact with. Practically speaking this means that God has a purpose for your family, for the ministry of which you are a part of for your city, and yes, for the nations.

Many Christians don't realize that secular humanism has done everything to root out everything that relates to God. It is a worldview that places total trust in mankind, believing that we are to look within ourselves and to each other to meet every need that we face in society. To believe that God is the center of the universe and our relationships is contrary and unnecessary to secular humanism. Therefore, when I look to God as the creator and designer, I am declaring a world view that says that all of life and its purpose comes from Him. He is the architect. He has a blueprint and I want to know what it is! Also, all of our blueprints interact with others in complex and intricate ways. These intersections are a part of our blueprint and have significant implications for our relationships and lives.

WALKING IT OUT

What does our life blueprint look like? How do we measure the Fivefold? How can I get use these practical steps to experience what this purpose is? This book is written out of the perspective of a practitioner, not a theorist. I have helped thousands of individuals and ministries walk out and apply the Fivefold as a part of a biblical culture. It is not my goal to review what I wrote in my previous book, but instead provide a practical manual and application tool. So, let's explore in the next chapter what a blueprint approach can do to accomplish the goal of "walking it out."

CHAPTER 2

THE STEPS TO READING A BLUEPRINT

WHAT IS A BLUEPRINT?

We all know that a blueprint is a drawing used for buildings and structures. However, it is far more than a simple and artistic drawing. The process of what we call a blueprint was developed in 1842, by a chemist named John Herschel. The process he created had the goal of alleviating the cumbersome process of hand tracing original drawings. It was a way to duplicate and make copies available of updated designs for those who follow the blueprints, beginning with an architect. After that there are building owners, project managers, construction workers, sub-contractors, and local governmental representatives that interpret the blueprints.

Without going into too much detail, I want to illustrate the arduous purpose that a blueprint serves. Every change in the design means an updated blueprint is necessary. It is the design process itself that ultimately articulates the exact measurements, materials, and execution of the plans on the blueprint.

READING A BLUEPRINT

For most of us laymen, a blueprint has many markings and notations that are unfamiliar. We can perhaps understand the dimensions, but there are important instructions that overlap with other blueprints and detailed plans. Personally, I have never built anything from a blueprint, and so I am not pretending to be an expert in any way.

In my research, there seems to be common steps to reading a blueprint. My source for the language to use in this book is my stepfather, John Kennelly, who worked as an engineer for 35 years. Most people are not familiar with how to read a blueprint, and I found it interesting to see the parallels to reading our spiritual blueprint. John is familiar with blueprints, and he has given input and corrections to keep this as accurate as possible. In fact, please read his notes after the preface to explain his approach to editing the book.

In the following pages I briefly describe the steps to reading a blueprint and adapt it to my analogy. There are six primary categories that have a chapter that relates to you reading the blueprint of your life.

It is my goal to assist every reader to have a better understanding of their call and purpose, as well as a basic plan to activate behavior toward the goals. Therefore, I am going to use the analogy of reading a blueprint to the steps of identifying and clarifying your destiny. In essence, I am seeking a measuring tool to assist people to mapping out their destiny.

Here are the Steps in the article referenced above that I have edited for this exercise:

STEP 1, READ THE TITLE BLOCK, (THE NAME, AUTHOR, NUMBER, LOCATION)

For now, let's call the Title Block, "Your Destiny", the author is the Holy Spirit. This book is about you, the reader, coming into your purpose and helping others to do so. Our goal however isn't to know our purpose, it is to experience it. For example, Ephesians 4:15-16 states the goal of equipping is to become mature and to come into the full measure of Christ. **Chapter 3, entitled "What is My Blueprint?",** I will help you answer this most fundamental question. The focus in this chapter is to discover both the primary and secondary Fivefold anointing that has been made available to you. Next comes the defining tools by adding your main passion and burden as it clarifies the direction for your life. In addition, it is vital to have a sense of the Holy Spirit leading, revealing, and confirming your call. The chapter will conclude with an assessment tool you can use to take the next step forward.

STEP 2: READ THE REVISION BLOCK

This is where the changes to the blueprint are listed. I want to emphasize: the blueprint isn't the building! It shows us the dimensions and nature of the building, but it is the process that brings the result. The blueprint isn't the focus, you are! Over time changes are necessary. Places and people change in our lives, but generally our purpose overall remains on a steady course. As it relates to the Fivefold there are different passions and burdens that God puts on our hearts. All these stages involve crucial clarifications. In **Chapter 4, "From Titles to Passion"**, you will explore what your destiny looks like as an expression. We need to make significant observations that get away from titles to defining the actual drivers and dreams that summarize our calling.

STEP 3: READ THE NOTES AND LEGENDS

This part of reading the blueprint has to do with aspects that refer to scale, symbols, and applicable specifications. For example, there are guidelines, local laws, and reminders for success. These are notes to help you be successful at your goal. As we grow in the Fivefold ministry, there are helpful guidelines that relate to assist us. As an example, there are many important principles that help you in the process of the interpretation and application of prophetic words. In **Chapter 5, "The Word as our Guide"**, you will discover your place in the context of the whole. This chapter will focus on the Fivefold function of the larger body and its benefits. As we recognize and honor the impact of others in our lives, we can see the whole building as it is designed to be. The goal is to be a part of what God is doing in you alongside others. The major notation is here, "Don't do this life by yourself!"

STEP 4: DETERMINE THE VIEW

With a blueprint there are three views in a 2D drawing: Plan, Elevation, and Sectional. The Plan View is a birds-eye-view from the top. The Elevation View is the perspective from the side. The Sectional View is a view from the inside and will show the inner workings and angles as it relates to other parts. These can show the opposite sides and also depicting height. In **Chapter 6, "Seeing through the Eyes of God and Others."** All too often we rely on our own viewpoint and wisdom. What does God's word say about you and your calling? How can you learn to listen to what others see for your life and purpose? The Plan View is God's plan, the Elevation is the view from others, and the Sectional View is the way that your life impacts others around you. This chapter will bring great freedom to build trust with others, and to invite the Holy Spirit to teach you about your anointing.

STEP 5: ESTABLISH THE SCALE

Blueprints are scaled down drawings and the measurement scale is crucial that everything is in proportion. In the spiritual realm we all have spheres of authority and areas of influence. **Chapter 7, "How to Measure Your Sphere of Authority"** helps explain the roles of authority and how to measure what God has assigned for you. Most problems in people's lives have to do with relationships and how our interaction and shared authority impacts our lives and destiny. It is crucial to know where your authority begins and ends, and being aware of how to honor others that you are called to be in relationship with. This practical chapter illustrates the importance of alignment, how authority increases or decreases, and how to properly measure what God has called you to release.

STEP 6: INSPECT THE GRID SYSTEM

On the perimeter of a blueprint there is an alpha numeric grid system so that users can identify specific objects and their location on the print. Example: a particular item may be found at zone 5D on the blueprint. This is true for your blueprint. **Chapter 8 is entitled, "Where is My Ministry?"** One of the greatest concerns people have is if they are in a church or ministry that doesn't recognize their call. What happens if those you are in covenant with don't understand in the Fivefold? This problem can exist in every sphere of our lives. We could feel as though we are misunderstood and don't belong anywhere. It is time to inspect the grid and see exactly how you are called to be positioned to others. Often it isn't those around us that need to change, it is our orientation and intentional awareness of our call. God has a sphere for you and in this chapter you will be to define and inspect what it is.

STEP 7: THE FINISH SCHEDULE

As you approach completion, it is time to look at the overall project, which can include appearance and appliances. The goal isn't to keep changing and changing, but rather to have a plan to complete and build it! **Chapter 9 is a hands-on guide called, "From Design to Destiny."** In this chapter there will be a declaration exercise that connects all the previous chapters into one powerful life statement. This will include helpful principles for not only individuals, but for churches and ministries alike. This is about the goal of coming into the fullness and maturity that Christ has for us. Included in this chapter is a case study of my own life as an example to inspire you as you write your own "DESTINY DECLARATION."

CHAPTER 3

WHAT IS MY BLUEPRINT?

WHAT IS MY PURPOSE?

A primary question thats everyone asks during their lifetime is, "What is my purpose? Why am I here and where am I going?" It is a fundamental yearning that we all have as we look beyond the demands of everyday life and meeting our basic needs. While it is very difficult to answer these questions broadly, I believe that an understanding of the Fivefold ministries is helpful in providing basic or skeletal answers to these questions. Do I really believe that knowing the essence of your Fivefold anointing can answer this question? Absolutely, and I have witnessed this while teaching on the topic around the world.

At the conclusion of a teaching at a conference on the Fivefold ministry, a 73-year-old woman came to me. She said, "I wish I had heard this message 50 years ago. I have always felt other people's burdens so deeply and I didn't know what to do with them. Sometimes it is so strong that I wake up in the middle of night praying for people, some of whom I hardly knew. Realizing this was both a pastoral and prophetic anointing shows me that this is how God designed me. It is an anointing and is directly related to my purpose." As we hugged for a moment, I was overwhelmed with God's joy in her. Her day of validation had come, she felt valued by God.

I have had the honor of hearing hundreds and perhaps thousands of similar testimonies over the decades. Nearly everyone wants to know who they are and how they have impacted others. Unfortunately, in the traditional church, it is primarily those with titles and formal roles that feel this validation. The Fivefold is not about those titles or positions as many have presented it. Rather it is much healthier and effective when we focus on the function of each of the Fivefold gifts and how we can release God's heart through these Fivefold anointings.

THE GOAL OF THE BLUEPRINT

This captures the motivation to define a blueprint for your life. The goal is to bring the reader into a greater sense of purpose, fulfillment, and direction. Our purpose is not just found in tasks and roles, but in who we are and what we are becoming. The goal is to define as clearly as possible who we are and the purpose that God has for us. Exactly as it says in Jeremiah, we can believe that God knew us before we were formed, and He appointed us into His purpose even before we were born. This belief has penetrated to the core of my being, and it is what motivates me to share with you the principles in this book. Please remember, the goal is not to know what your primary and Fivefold anointings are, but to initiate a deeper realization of what your purpose is. Certainly, this realization does not complete the blueprint, but for me it is foundational and crucial in understanding the larger picture.

THE ROLE OF THE FIVEFOLD IN THE BLUEPRINT

If the goal is discovering who we were created to be, then we must find tools that assist us and help us draw the blueprint for us. Unlike the gifts of the Spirit in I Corinthians 12, Ephesians 4:7 tells us emphatically, "But to each one of us grace has been given as Christ apportioned it." What I love about this verse is that it includes all of us, "to each one." There is no one who is left out! That is exciting because everyone can know they are included in God's plan. It also accentuates that we all belong to Him and are created by Him.

THE DIFFERNCE BETWEEN THE GIFTS OF THE SPIRIT AND FIVEFOLD

We are familiar with I Corinthians 12 which speaks of nine spiritual gifts. In that chapter the Greek word for gifts is "charisma." Strong's Greek Concordance defines the word as a spiritual gift or divine endowment. I Corinthians 12:7 clarifies this further and calls the gift a "manifestation of the Holy Spirit." This is an expression or bestowment. That is an amazing reality, the Holy Spirit expresses His will and person through us. We call them the "Gifts of the Spirit" because of this. They belong to the Spirit and are released and realized according to His will and purpose.

The word for the Fivefold anointings in Ephesians 4:7 has the same root word as gifts, "Charis", but is often translated as "grace." A grace has been given to you. Strong's Greek Concordance says this: "a manner or act."

The definition continues that it is the "divine influence upon the heart...and reflection in the life." In other words, it is a part of your being, and it influences your actions, heart, and reflects who you are. This is like how we use the word "graciousness," which, by the way, is one of the meanings of "charis" in the Greek.

I want to impress this point, that grace is given to you. It is part of your entire being and was woven into your fabric as God formed you and set you apart. When we say a person is gracious, or they have a grace (for the poor for example) we are stating something about the personhood. It is a description of a core attribute that a person has.

So the difference that is very important is, unlike the Gifts of the Spirit, this grace belongs to you. It is a part of who you are created to be. This is why I call it part of the blueprint. It is an aspect of your design, and it gives framework to who you are created to be! If this is true, don't you want to understand what this grace is even more than before? More personally, don't you want to know the grace that has been given to you?

WHO GIVES US THIS GRACE?

First, isn't it wonderful that we have a special grace? What makes it even more special is that grace is from Christ himself. You see that in verse 7, it says, "according to the measure of the gift of Christ." (KJV). The reason I quote this version as it explicitly states the word "gift" which is from the Greek word, "dorea." The grace we are referring to is a gift from Christ. It is directly from our Savior and Messiah. That is why the Fivefold gifts are sometimes called the "gifts of Jesus", as compared to the "gifts of the Spirit."

STARTING THE STEPS OF THE BLUEPRINT

In the last chapter, I listed the seven steps to complete and express our personal blueprint. With excitement, we are now ready to start examining what these steps are.

STEP 1: READ THE TITLE BLOCK

As we read the title block, we see the title of the project and the name of the author. In this analogy, the creation has our name on it, and the author is God. In Psalms 139:13-15 David wrote, "You formed my innermost being, shaping my delicate inside and my intricate outside, and wove them all together in my mother's womb. I thank you, God, for making me so mysteriously complex! Everything you do is marvelously breathtaking. It simply amazes me to think about it! How thoroughly you know me, Lord! You even formed every bone in my body when you created me in the secret place; carefully, skillfully you shaped me from nothing to something." (The Passion Translation)

God is the author, and He does have an exact plan for our lives, a blueprint that He intricately formed and wove us together. It is vital to remember that we are His idea. We are His created being. This is something to celebrate in a day where identity and even gender are in question.

THE TITLE BLOCK IN PRACTICAL TERMS

In Christ, we have specific and measurable gifts and graces that are in the basic drawings of who we are. Our blueprint can partly be read by understanding and defining what these gifts and graces are. Because this is more of a manual and practical book, I want you to pause for a moment. I ask you to believe and then declare out loud, "Jesus has released specific graces and gifts into my life, and I choose to pursue as to what those are and what that means for my life and purpose." If you declared that over your life, you just took a step toward your destiny. You have examined the "TITLE BLOCK."

THIS GRACE IS MEASURED

Perhaps the fact that this grace is measured by Christ is why I use the illustration of a blueprint. Let's go back to Ephesians 4:7 and look at this word used for measure or size, "And He has generously given each one of us supernatural grace, according to the size of the gift of Christ." (Ephesians 4:7 TPT) In the Greek the word translated "size" here is "metron." A "metron" literally means measure or measurement. According to Strong's Concordance it implies that it is limited or not without limits. Measurements are vital to understanding the blueprint for your life. We have a beginning and an end.

For me this truth has created an insatiable hunger to know that this measure is. I want to know the grace and gifts God has given to me, but just as important, I want to know what the measure is, and the scope. Since Christ measured them out, it is important that I am seeking to walk in the fullness of this measure. That is exactly what Ephesians 4:13 speaks about, coming into the "full measure" (NIV).

CHAPTER 3 | WHAT IS MY BLUEPRINT?

Recently I bought a television for one of my sons for Christmas. The measurement was everything. How big should it be, 55", 65", or even 75'? As of this writing you can buy a 98" UHD TV for around $4,000. I remember when a 32" tv was considered standard. Now, 50" is considered small by many people.

To know the measure is to realize the sphere God has given to us. It is those realms of influence that we are called to as a part of expressing our purpose. This is the topic of Chaper 7, "Understanding Your Authority." At this time, I want to stir a deeper desire to know the grace given to you by Christ, and also the measure. I don't want half of what God has prepared for me, I want it all. What about you, how much do you want to know the graces given to you and what the measurements are?

WHAT ARE THESE GRACES OR GIFTS?

Perhaps it is implied but is important for me to say the Bible to me is inspired by the Holy Spirit and is authoritative in my life as a follower of Christ. I love the Word of God and it is vital that we let the Bible speak for itself. So, to comprehend the grace that is measured we need to go to the context of Ephesians 4. I explain this in my book on the Fivefold, but for new readers this must be said again.

If you look at the context of Ephesians 4:7-10, we discussed that Christ gives measured gifts, then vs 8-10 are a commentary of the how Psalm 68:18 tells us that Christ will ascend and give us gifts. All three verses explain the source of these gifts. Then vs. 11 picks up from vs. 7 and says, "And he has appointed some *with grace* to be apostles, and some *with grace* to be prophets, and some *with grace* to be evangelists, and some *with grace* to be pastors, and some *with grace* to be teachers. (The Passion Translation.) I love how the Passion Translation captures that "some with the grace to be." So here we have a list of five graces, and they identify them in terms of a function. Many people interpret these to be titles, and while I don't reject this interpretation, a grace is by definition more of an act or demonstration. I believe that we have lost something by rushing to titles too quickly, and not realizing the more important, "But to each one of us a grace has been given..." There I said it, everyone has Fivefold graces within their life. In traditional Pentecostalism, the Fivefold was limited to only those who have a call to an office. I wholeheartedly disagree with this. I take literally the "to each one of us."

This is the main reason the Fivefold has been misunderstood, and I believe extremely limited and even restricted. The greatest titles we have are son and daughter, brother and sister, and the greatest among us is a "servant." In our identity and purpose we can't seek the title as the goal, it is to walk in unity, to become mature lovers of Christ, and to move into the full measure Christ has for us. This is explicitly stated in Ephesians 4:13, "until we all reach unity in the faith and in the knowledge of the Son of God and become mature, attaining to the whole measure of the fullness of Christ." (NIV)

So here we come to another moment of declaration. We aren't looking for titles and positions, we are looking to fulfill our purpose and destiny in Christ! To know this we need to affirm that each one of us, including ourselves, have received a measured grace. The Fivefold is not for

CHAPTER 3 | WHAT IS MY BLUEPRINT?

the super spiritual, but for every one of us. This is true for each of us and the blueprint of our destiny must include this.

HOW DO WE KNOW WHAT GRACE WE RECEIVED?

We can identify the traits and characteristics of each of the Fivefold graces. A great portion of my book, The Five Fingers of God, goes through each of the graces explaining in detail what they are and the attributes I have discovered that accompany and reflect upon each one. Without over spiritualizing it, we can look at the fruit, desires, passion, and burdens that you have, and this often reveals easily what your primary and secondary graces are. The reason I put it this way is because I have found that we are not made from a cookie cutter, but we are uniquely and wonderfully made. As I have trained people around the world in this endeavor, I often found that a combination of two graces was effective in describing your blueprint for your life. At the end of this chapter there is a Fivefold assessment tool that helps you identify where you measure yourself in all the Fivefold graces. Based on experience, it was developed to give you a glimpse of your primary and secondary anointing graces. The goal is not to pigeonhole you or put you in a box. On the contrary, the goal is to give you freedom. This will help in reading the block on your blueprint.

THE ROLE OF THE PRIMARY AND SECONDARY ANOINTINGS

The primary anointing is your main motivator and driving force. It is the impetus inside that makes respond to life and people as you do. It is how God made you. It is far deeper than a personality trait. It is a grace that Christ himself gave to you to fulfill your call and purpose. The secondary is the complementary grace that directs how you express your primary anointing. I like to call it the flavor, like the seasoning on a steak or a BBQ rub. It adds definition and clarification of your primary.

For example, the apostolic is first, or primary, and the prophetic anointing is second, or secondary. My primary passion is to equip and train people in discovering their destiny and purpose. A great deal of my ministry has been dedicated to this goal. When I am sent to a group of people in different nations, the Lord gives me a prophetic voice of love and encouragement to open the hearts of the people to my primary message. The Spirit even told me that this was the approach I was to take wherever I went. When I prophesy, the Spirit shows me a person's calling and often the attack that tries to thwart the calling on their life. As I have grown in interpreting and sharing these prophetic insights, it has had a major impact for individuals, families, ministries, churches, and movements.

As I grabbed on to these and articulated these graces, the purpose of my life has become clearer and clearer. Many times, the words not only revealed the purpose, but specific direction and application of how to fulfill my call has resulted. What an amazing process and gift. That is why I call it the Fivefold blueprint. It isn't the building, but the clarity that has resulted has been measurable.

On the following pages there is a Fivefold Assessment Tool to assist you in discovering your primary and secondary anointings. After that there is a short description of the Fivefold graces and then a list of attributes. Circle the ones that you think describe you. There is also some space to add characteristics that aren't listed. Once this is prepared you will be ready to take the next step in defining your destiny.

A digital tool for this may be found on my new website, www.blueprintforyourdestiny.com. Please note that this tool is in process and is not available at time of publishing this book, but will be completed at a later time.

THE FIVEFOLD GIFT ASSESSMENT TOOL

The profile includes thirty pairs of statements. Read each pair and **choose the one** that better reflects your preferences. Then, in the column, circle the letter that corresponds with the statement you choose.

No	Statements	A	B	C	D	E
1	I seek to align myself with apostolic leaders and movements					
	I like to walk out problems with people				D	
2	I ask God specific questions to get specific answers		B			
	I like to articulate truth and make it practical for people to understand					E
3	I want to know if someone is saved or not	A				
	I expect people to mature and grow			C		
4	People regularly seek me out for counsel and support				D	
	I like to be as accurate as possible in all I do					E
5	I write down visions and dreams on a regular basis		B			
	I think about different approaches to sharing the gospel with others			C		
6	I am told I have a lot of discernment of the spiritual things		B			
	Being biblical is essential in the way I live my life					E
7	I believe unity is the main way to make a difference	A				
	I believe hearing God and knowing his will is the way to make a difference		B			
8	I tend to see things as either black or white					E
	I have the ability to keep the big picture in the forefront	A				
9	I tend to be truth centered					E
	I have a heart for the lost and pray about this often			C		
10	I like to help people mature and make equipping a priority	A				
	I love to heal and minister to people's hearts				D	

CHAPTER 3 | WHAT IS MY BLUEPRINT?

#	Statement	A	B	C	D	E
11	I have wept for the lost on occasion			C		
	I like to equip others to grow and increase	A				
12	I love to listen and ask people questions				D	
	I like to help people hear God for themselves		B			
13	Bringing people into their destiny is the most important thing there is	A				
	Loving people is the most important thing there is				D	
14	I seek to hear God for others regularly		B			
	I don't want to be judgmental, but people have to be honest with themselves					E
15	I often pray for miracles and see people healed	A				
	I am passionate about keeping people accountable and in the truth					E
16	I have an inquisitive mind when I am studying					E
	I often hear and see things for others when I pray		B			
17	People tell me that I am very patient and caring				D	
	I love to reach out on the street and other non-church settings			C		
18	I like to network and bridge people	A				
	I assist people to interpret dreams and visions		B			
19	I like to be learn everything I can about a topic					E
	I am a peace-maker and show people how to forgive				D	
20	I love to comfort and encourage people				D	
	I am consistent in praying for the lost			C		
21	I often give personal words to encourage others		B			
	I carry people in my heart even if I met them only once				D	
22	I love the gospel and share it every time I can			C		
	I focus on people groups and think of strategies to reach them	A				
23	I see people in sin and think immediately, "they just need Jesus."			C		
	I am very quick to feel compassion even if it is a movie character!				D	

24	I articulate declarations from the Spirit and declare them over people and groups		B			
	I love to share anything that is important to me with everyone			C		
25	I notice when people aren't at meetings or events and pray for their well-being				D	
	I am very aware of the connection between the natural and spiritual realms		B			
26	I focus on foundational truths and principles					E
	I like to meet new people and be in new situations			C		
27	I like to start new things and recruit others to assist me	A				
	Having daily fresh revelation is important to me		B			
28	I eagerly share my faith when the occasion arises			C		
	I like to put things into order and clarity					E
29	People come to me for support and help				D	
	I like to train others and see them released	A				
30	I help people stay truthful to their stated purpose					E
	I invite people to come with me to church or other settings			C		
	Total each column. All 5 columns should equal 30 totaled together.					

Take the total from each of the columns from the previous page and plot them on this graph, by placing a dot in the middle of the square that represents your score for each column. Then you can connect each dot with a line creating a line chart or shade in the column in starting at the bottom of the chart an stopping at your dot representing your score for each column.

CHAPTER 3 | WHAT IS MY BLUEPRINT?

No	A	B	C	D	E
12					
11					
10					
9					
8					
7					
6					
5					
4					
3					
2					
1					

Key: Each column presents the following gift.

A = Apostolic
B = Prophetic
C = Evangelistic
D = Pastoral
E = Teacher(istic!)

Which Fivefold Gift did you receive the most points for? This is your primary Fivefold Gift. The column with the second highest points represents your secondary Fivefold Gift.

My primary Fivefold Gift is: _____.

My Secondary Fivefold Gift is: _____.

CHAPTER 4
THE DESTINY EQUATION

STEP 2, READ THE REVISION BLOCK

The next step in reading a blueprint is, READ THE REVISION BLOCK. This is where changes, definitions, and intrinsic goals are preserved by making revisions along the way. We all would love to have an easy formula to come into our destiny, but at the same time we all know it is the journey. Even the best plans need to be altered to execute. In buildings, perhaps the materials we wanted become unavailable or go up in price. Laws that require widening entry ways or making ramps for the handicapped can alter the plans and costs significantly. This is also true as you seek to fulfill your purpose. There will be new information that leads to adjustments in our lives. Many of these will be minor, others can be huge.

Recently I had a significant scare with my health. Due to a recent trip to the Philippines and Japan, I had a streak where we traveled 54 hours in four days either in a car or plane. In addition, we sat in meetings and at meals. As a result, I got blood clots in my legs and it traveled to my lungs. Wow, I had a saddle pulmonary embolism as well as many blood clots on both sides of my lungs. I genuinely feel this was an attack of the enemy against the impact we are having in nations. What do I do with this information, does it impact my destiny? It sure challenges my ability to travel as well as other details in planning and building. Along the way, we need to make adjustments that are specific and tangible.

Over the years people have completed gift and Fivefold assessments, but often they put it in a drawer and there is no follow-up. This is why we need to read and add to the Revision Block.

Regarding the actual blueprint for our destiny, I have added some new information to the way the Fivefold is presented. The result of this new perspective has led to a helpful equation that brings this to the point of clarification. We need more information added to our Fivefold gifts.

Here is the equation that has emerged:

FIVEFOLD + PASSION + BURDEN = DESTINY

After completing the Fivefold assessment tool, a second approach assists in taking this to the next level. When I have done this actively in ministry the results have been exciting. The addition of two basic questions bring great clarity for people as they seek their destiny. The first question is, "What is your passion?" and second, "What is the burden on your heart?" I have found that asking these questions often reveal a specific task, group of people, a place of influence, or a focus in ministry.

Let me illustrate. My wife Ann is Prophetic (Primary) and Pastoral (Secondary.) Now let's add the next part of the equation. What is her passion. That is very clear by her life, it is intimacy with God and to be a part of releasing His glory through intercession. Her burden for others is to help people experience God's love and presence for themselves. Wow, do you see how those next two questions really added to the larger blueprint picture? The answers took the anointings and then put this into practical action.

The Destiny Assessment tool that you will complete later in this book will start with your Fivefold graces, and then add your passion and burden. Through this simple equation, you will get insight and hopefully revelation into your calling. This tool is designed to help you be as specific as possible and to bring as much current definition as you can. This is what READ THE REVISIONS means when studying a blueprint. It tells you practical implications and even intangibles that are revealed in the process that were not clear when the design process began.

WHAT IS YOUR PASSION?

When I ask people this question, I get a widely spread response. Some people know right away what to say. For others they have a more general sense. Yet, there are those who state they really don't know. That is why we need to READ THE REVISIONS. It is time to add and maybe even subtract in this situation. We can add by learning to speak what really gets us excited. Other times we need to get rid of distractions and things that hinder our purpose. We don't want to be put in a box, which is why the freedom to revise and further clarify can be life giving. I have found that a person's passions and burdens can both clarify and define.

As I said, for some the light goes on for them as it relates to the Fivefold graces. When asked about their passion, common responses are, "I love to bring comfort and healing to people's hearts," or, "My passion is to help others hear God for themselves," and, "My main passion is to equip people into what God has created them for." Those are each a Fivefold grace in action. The first of healing hearts is pastoral, helping people hear God is prophetic, and equipping for destiny is apostolic. If you ask and listen to people about their main passion it will begin aligning with and expanding the Fivefold graces. It will be traction to the tires of movement.

Other people seemed to have less clarity by being too general or not knowing at all. That is alright, but now it is time to search our hearts, to listen to the Spirit, and to seek the Lord for new insights. Sometimes I encourage people to think of other people or ministries that really stir them. By this example, you get in touch with the passion inside of you.

For me, one of my main passions is to observe people making major breakthrough. Many people feel stuck or minimize their giftings. I genuinely believe everyone is anointed by the Holy Spirit! I don't like to say one person is really anointed when the truth is all of us are. As a result, I have developed numerous messages on the topics of anointing, and on breakthrough. It is a great passion that has turned into a significant aspect of my ministry. This passion goes hand in hand with the apostolic and prophetic, and I get to watch people have breakthroughs as they minister and align themselves with us.

I can give many examples of this, but my favorite is taking people to Kenya on a transformation trip and send them out like Jesus in pairs (or often in groups of three or four people.) On our trip to Kenya in 2023 a woman told me she didn't know how to pray for people let alone prophesy with them. The Lord showed me the immense compassion she felt for others, and that was all she needed to focus on. She is Pastoral/Evangelistic, but at that time those words meant very little. However, she could agree that she wanted to share the compassion and love of Jesus. That's all she needed as the Holy Spirit filled her with love and it flowed so freely to the people. It took only a couple of days for her to go to a whole new level of ministry expression just by embracing her passion from God.

WHAT IS YOUR BURDEN?

While this question is similar, I have found it solicits a different response. A burden is something that God puts on our hearts for others that results in an outcome. It can sound like the goal of our passion and it too reveals a clear part of our purpose mission. It is also different in that it defines the outcome from our perseverance. Doing our passion sounds more fun, but often a burden is what causes us to become proactive and more deeply involved with people.

Earlier I expressed that my burden is to bring people into maturity and calling. For me, this burden can be disappointing and exciting at the same time. First, I am often amazed at how people can attend a church or be a Christian for decades without being challenged to mature or discover their calling. Secondly, it is exciting to see how people can shift quickly when in the right environment and setting.

A burden is something you carry and feel, it is not meant to crush or defeat you. It is a part of your calling and flows out of your passion. They are related, but the burden is more expression and task oriented than your passion is. Let me give a further example. You can have a passion for people to hear God's voice, but your burden is that they really come to a place to place where they can receive His love in a deeper and deeper way. The passion is your driver, but the burden is the follow through.

For me my burden is illustrated by helping people identify what is holding them back. A lot of people have a sense of their call and purpose, but they are held back by insecurities, rejection, or lack of direction. My burden is to help people get past false expectations, wounding from leaders, and lack of direction.

Even though we will look at this in detail as we do the Destiny Declaration in chapter 9, let's pray and make some notes here.

What is your main driving passion? You can list 4-6 things here (or more if you would like):

What are your main burdens for others that you believe are on your heart from the Lord? You can list 4-6 things here (if they overlap or repeat you can refine this later):

CHAPTER 5
THE WORD AS OUR GUIDE

STEP 3: READ THE NOTES AND LEGENDS

The notes and legends that are there for context and perspective. These notes are there to remind us of variables that are impacting but not directly seen in the drawings. The notes have to do with ordinances, codes, and factors that we need to follow as we build. These are often non-negotiable as they relate to laws or limits that are inherent to the design.

THE WORD OF GOD IS OUR GUIDE

When it comes to our destiny and purpose, we have stated that God is the author. He has also given us the Holy Bible, the written word to guide us in all things. In the Scriptures we can discover not only who God is, but who we are. First, as we focus on Him, we learn the incredible love that God has for us.

In the written word we find our identity as sons and daughters of God. We can't understand our destiny and purpose without learning who we are from the Bible. There are many books dedicated to this.

In other words, everything in the design is informed by

the Word of God as the standard. Nothing in our calling should contradict God's character and nature revealed in His word. These are the notes so to speak, and the legends are spiritual principles that are intrinsic to the design of God.

JESUS' BAPTISM, TEMPTATION, AND NAZARETH

Nothing illustrates this more for me than the progression that Jesus goes through as He entered His destiny. We believe and understand that while on earth Jesus was fully man and fully God. It is important to embrace the deity of Jesus, but at times I think we downplay the reality of the battle that Jesus faced as being fully man. It wasn't a cake walk or slam dunk. Jesus had real battles, temptations, and choices. We see this clearly in the interactions with his mother Mary, while in the wilderness, and in the Garden of Gethsemane. The reason I state this is because it can be encouraging to us as we walk and grow toward our destiny. Jesus clung to the words of His father, and they were what defined His ministry and expression.

This is true for your life. The Notes and Legends are where you get your identity, whom you listen to, how you live in accountability, and how you express your calling.

This is powerfully observed in Jesus call and the start of His ministry in baptism.

THREE EVENTS THAT LAUNCHED JESUS' MINISTRY

It is hard to fathom that Jesus did not begin His public ministry until He was 30 years old. This was primarily due to the Jewish culture that did not consider a person to be mature until 30 years. Regardless, we often feel pressure at a much earlier age to be effective. I graduated from Seminary when I was 23 years old and went into full time ministry. Wow, what a learning curve that was. This said, there is something to be said about Jesus waiting until this age. There was no rush, it was all about the Father's timing. The foundation for Jesus was knowing the heart of the Father. This would be paramount and to Jesus' entire ministry.

I wish this were a more fundamental requirement for anyone entering the ministry. In a blueprint the notes and legends make sure certain guidelines, laws, and principles are included into the build plan. The same is true with our lives in order for us to be effective and fruitful. No awareness of our call is greater than our knowing the heart of the Father for us.

THE BAPTISM OF JESUS

This truth is illustrated so powerfully in the baptism of Jesus. In Mark 1:11 it says, "At the same time, a voice spoke from heaven, saying: "You are my Son, my cherished one, and my greatest delight is in you!" (TPT)

When speaking, I like to draw attention to this powerful verse by saying the wrong thing. For example, "This is my son who will die for everyone's sin", or "This is my son who will perform many miracles." I do this to show that instead of focusing on what Jesus would do, the Father focuses on the importance and delight He has in His Son, Jesus. His focus was on the person Jesus, not the ministry of Jesus.

This is where our destiny must flow from. It really is about our relationship with God. One danger of religion is that it replaces relationship with rituals and rules. We can try to earn God's love without realizing it. We can make our focus on what we do for God, instead of knowing His heart and will for us.

I often listen to people to see what kind of language they use when referring to God. Without knowing, some people use words that reflect guilt, shame, and striving. They express that they can do so much more and never measure up. In part, it is true that we can always do more and we will never be perfect.

When someone feels profoundly and deeply loved they sound and act differently. There is a security and peace that exudes from their life and ministry. I honestly don't allow guilt or shame to drive me in anyway. The reason is that it doesn't work or create good fruit in me.

Everyone must examine whether they have experienced what Jesus did in His baptism. We desperately need to hear for ourselves that we are loved, cherished, and called by name.

Jesus knew the Father's love and approval before His ministry began. For me, learning to experience God's love has become the main activity in my spiritual life. With His love, I can impact nations. Without it, I can be religious and self-righteous. Again, the notes and legends are about the intrinsic implications that are within the design itself.

THE TEMPATION OF JESUS

The second event that ushered Jesus into His calling was

the temptation in the wilderness immediately following his baptism. I have learned in helping people discover their call that the enemy attacks the anointing. This is because the power of God is released as we walk in what the Lord has prepared for us.

Often, I make a joke, "Didn't Jesus have time to be tempted before the baptism?" I'm trying to point out that something amazing happened in the waters of baptism. This was the initiation of Jesus into public ministry, and the Holy Spirit came upon Him like a dove. Thus, the Bible tells us in Matthew 4:1, "Afterward, the Holy Spirit led Jesus into the lonely wilderness in order to reveal His strength against the accuser by going through the ordeal of testing." (TPT). I find it very significant that Jesus was led into the wilderness as a precursor to Jesus' ministry. It is an important step to understand the anointing we receive from the Holy Spirit.

THE ATTACK IS AGAINST OUR CALLING

I am a firm believer that when we start to realize and come into our call, the enemy does everything he can to derail and deceive us. Jesus three temptations had something in common, to rely on His own wisdom and to use the newly received power to serve His own needs. The response was the same in essence, "I look to my God, my Father" in everything.

In my previous books I spent a great deal of time explaining the significance of our anointing. I John 2:27 has become a life verse for me, "But the wonderful anointing you have received from God *is so much greater than their deception and* now lives in you. There's no need for anyone to keep teaching you. His anointing teaches you all that you need to know, for it will lead you into truth, not a counterfeit. So just as the anointing has taught you, remain in him." (TPT) This verse is not saying we don't need teachers for training, it is reminding us that the anointing we have is from God and it is greater than the temptations that try to deceive us. The truth is that we can trust the Holy Spirit to lead and guide us if we remain and listen. We aren't alone, but the anointing will teach us how to rely on the Holy Spirit and not our own strength. Teachers can reveal and explain doctrine, but the anointing confirms the leading of the Spirit and obedience. The notes and legend say, "Trust the Holy Spirit to lead you!"

YOU CAN UNDERSTAND YOUR DESTINY BY THE TEMPTATIONS YOU RECEIVE

Here is another amazing truth. Since the enemy attacks what is important, you can get a glimpse into your destiny through the attack. In my "FIVE FINGERS OF GOD" book there an entire chapter dedicated to this. For my purpose as step-by-step guide, you can ask yourself what the main attacks are in your life. As you list them, you can see how the enemy seeks to steal, kill, and destroy. For example, if your heart is wounded all the time, that is an attack against the pastoral anointing. The temptation is to shut people out instead of taking risks and letting them in. Teachers are often derailed and tempted by injustices. Also, if you look at the passions and burdens from the last chapter, you can see how these are related to the attack in your life. The enemy does not want you to feel effective or fruitful.

Jesus had a destiny to save the world, so the enemy

tempted Him to save himself with food, power, and control. None of these took Jesus out of the desire to look to the Father in everything. In fact, Jesus saw the power of the anointing to overcome and walk in trust and obedience. He knew the truth, and the anointing of that set Him free.

DECLARATION IN NAZARETH

The third station of Jesus release into ministry was in Nazareth. Before visiting Israel I hadn't realized that the village had probably only 200-300 residents at the time of Jesus childhood. That is smaller than many of the churches I have been in. This means that most people knew Jesus as a growing child, teenager, and man in his 20's. He ate in their homes, played games in the fields, made furniture with his father Joseph, and grew side by side with them. In Luke 4:14-17 we are told what happened after the wilderness, "Then Jesus, armed with the Holy Spirit's power, returned to Galilee, and His fame spread throughout the region. He taught in the synagogues and they glorified Him. When He came to Nazareth, where He had been raised, He went into the synagogue, as He always did on the Sabbath day. When Jesus came to the front to read the Scriptures, they handed Him the scroll of the prophet Isaiah." (TPT)

When Jesus left the wilderness, he headed to Galilee and to his hometown, Nazareth. I believe that this journey from the wilderness to Nazareth was a plan to not only challenge the people of his hometown, but also where Jesus would make a declaration against the fear of man and the unbelief that he faced regarding who He was. He knew the people wanted to see physical miracles, but His desire was to declare a greater miracle. He wanted to declare that He had been transformed by the anointing of the Holy Spirit, and with that He had the power to walk in five different anointings. I teach that these are the Fivefold ministries in the language of the function.

"The Spirit of the Lord is on me!" he declared. Not only that but this anointing has a purpose. He is quoting Isaiah 61 and it is recorded in Luke 4:18-19. (I quote it in the NIV because I've preached this so many times.) He proclaimed with boldness; I am anointed to:

Preach good news to the poor (evangelism)
Proclaim freedom for the prisoners (teaching)
Recovery of sight for the blind (prophetic)
Set the oppressed free (pastoral)
Proclaim the year of the Lord's favor (apostolic decree)

It is important to note that the anointing had specific focuses and functions. The same is true for you and is foundational to the premises in this book. God has a measured and pinpointed purpose for your anointings and gifts. These are given to you as you are created and later come into an expression as you walk into the Holy Spirit. These belong to you. Romans 11:29 says, "And when God chooses someone and graciously imparts gifts to him, they are never rescinded." (TPT) These gifts are inherently integrated into your whole being.

YOUR BLUEPRINT HAS ALL THREE OF JESUS' INITIATIONS

As this chapter is about the notes and legends, this process of coming into our destiny must include the way Jesus did:

1. An encounter of God's love that overwhelms us

2. Overcoming the temptation to use our anointings to serve our own needs and desires

3. The declaration against the fear and control of others that says, "The Spirit of the Lord is upon me for a purpose, and the purpose is...!"

We will declare these three aspects in our Destiny Declaration in chapter 9. These notes and legends are in our building block and are infused into all we are and what we do.

THE ROLE OF EQUIPPING TO DISCOVER OUR PURPOSE

I want to speak to the broader context of the Word of God as it relates to equipping. This next section could be the topic of its own book. I must admit something here. I have been teaching on equipping in a wrong way. Perhaps it's a short sighted, or a more shallow way if that helps you understand my heart.

Over the years I have taught on the Fivefold ministry with the primary goal of equipping. I have focused on Ephesians 4:12 as the main purpose of these graces. It says, "to equip his people for works of service, so that the body of Christ may be built up." For many of us the phrase "to equip his people" has become so common that it has become more of a generic ideal than a measurable reality. Of course, we all associate this with equipping, but what does that really mean?

Later on I explain the relational aspect of this word translated to equip. For now, let's focus on what the purpose of the equipping is. The goal of the five-fold leadership is to prepare people for works for service or literally, ministry. However, we stopped too early as we read the verses. I'll explain in a moment.

WORKS OF MINISTRY

God created us in part to have a ministry. This is a function that is supported by the identity, gifts, character, and personality that He has given to us. Our ministry flows out of who we are. That is who He has designed us to be. Works are exactly that: jobs, roles, tasks, and deeds that are characteristic of our ministry. We all have a "God designed" job description. I love how Ephesians 2:10 put this, "Even before we were born, God planned in advance our destiny and the good works we would do to fulfill it." (TPT)

BUILDING UP THE BODY

Fitting in with the analogy of the blueprint, we find in our notes and legends that we are called to build up the body of Christ. The Greek word for building can be translated "a structure." In this case it is building up, that is edifying and enhancing the body of Christ. That is the church. We are all called to be a part of something bigger than ourselves. God has a blueprint for the church and we are a part of the bigger picture. Our blueprints intersect with the larger body of Christ.

WHY DO WE STOP WITH VS. 12?

In recent years, I have realized that we stopped too soon! The power of Ephesians 4:12-13 outlines in detail what equipping looks like practicality. If you keep reading, vs. 13 says, "until we all reach unity in the faith and in the knowledge of the Son of God and become mature, attaining to the whole measure of the fullness of Christ." (NIV) In the Greek manuscripts there is no punctuation, but if you look in the English translations there are no periods, just commas. As I have sought to underscore what equipping is, verse 13 has become such an inspiration on how to equip the saints.

To understand this, we need to see equipping the people for works of ministry in the five following ways.

1. Build up the Body of Christ (servanthood)
2. Reach unity in the faith (relationship training)
3. In the knowledge of the Son of God (intimacy)
4. Become mature (character development)
5. Attain the Full Measure (destiny training!)

EQUIP TO BUILD THE BODY OF CHRIST

I missed it, this is all about relationships. We are not just parts of a body; we belong to each other and are called to build one another up. We are not islands and isolated from interdependence with others. We know this in theory, but often we find working with others to be more discouraging than positive. Relationships are not always easy, expectations are not always realistic, and disappointment can occur when we don't feel fruitful. The goal then is unity, but to be more accurate, unity in the faith. This is a major key as unity happens through our faith in Christ. He is the One that breaks down dividing walls and calls into relationships. Often what hinders people the most is that they experience disunity and division. Nothing kills the life and vitality of any ministry more than discord.

EQUIPPING PEOPLE ON THE ROLE OF UNITY

The truth is that many people don't come into a sense of purpose and often cite the relational conflicts and hindrances as a major reason. This is double sided however, because sometimes the partnership and synergy with others is the missing piece that we need to go to another level.

I am not just referring to the absence of conflict or division as the goal. True unity is far more proactive and intentional. Unity is teamwork, honor, cooperation, and respect. It embodies the ability to work through conflicts and to overcome relational obstacles. Unity is a relational IQ word.

This revelation is changing my whole perspective. In our equipping we have neglected to train people on how to have relationships. This involves learning how to build, maintain, and foster community. Think about it, what brings the most joy and yet pain in our lives? Most of us would agree it is relationships.

Taking this further, it has often been the inability to be unified in relationships that has hindered our calling. It may have wounded us and others to the degree that people withdraw their efforts and affections.

A blueprint must ultimately be viewed from a whole and unified perspective. All the parts relate to the entire project.

EQUIP ON HOW TO HANDLE CONFLICT

Over the course of the years, we have had training on marriage, parenting, and networking. Now is the time that we make relational a perspective for leadership. We need to help people measure their ability to work through relational issues and to be leaders of creating and maintaining unity. It is hard to admit, but a lot of people that we make our leaders don't have a track record of working through conflict. Instead of working through issues, many people just leave and go to another church or circle of friends. If you ask people why the relationships break down, the answers are quite common. They answer, "I didn't feel valued," "My opinion didn't matter", and "It seems like the leader already made the decision before coming to me."

Power struggles, distrust, and the need for control are all things that can impede our relationships. We can learn new skills and become mature leaders so that we can get beyond these obstacles. These are just over simplified comments, but at times I am stunned how even very loyal people choose to opt out because the conflict is too intimidating. People run away from conflict because they lack the skills to work through the issues. Let's change that!

THE ENEMY WANTS TO ISOLATE YOU

How does this apply to your destiny and the Fivefold? If we take Ephesians 4:13 literally it says, "until we all reach unity in the faith." That is a reality that is on God's heart and is at the core of Jesus prayer for all of us in John 17. It is a challenge to keep unity as a core value. The reason is that the enemy wants to alienate and isolate people from each other and from leaders. We need to become experts at recognizing the "notes and legends", that is the bigger picture issues that have to do with relational integrity.

One of my roles as a leader is to become involved in church conflicts. These include issues between pastors and their leaders but can be even broader as tensions arise between factions within the ministry. Regardless of the issues, it comes down to a relational breakdown somewhere. I have looked for a technical term, but the most useful word I have found is "weird." When I ask a group that is experiencing division, "When did it get weird?", most often people can articulate it rather quickly. Usually it is a misunderstanding, a false expectation, or when there is a perceived slight or disregard. Issues and disagreements are valid and real, so I don't want to minimize or oversimplify this. However, the bottom line is that the result is often division, but worse yet, isolation. The enemy's goal is to not only divide the relationship, but more acutely, to alienate you.

UNITY OF THE FAITH

At this point we don't know what to do, and we don't always know how to articulate ourselves well. Sometimes as leaders we feel responsible not only for ourselves so in our minds we are obligated to act. I have witnessed this repeatedly, where leaders get pushed into the middle and the weight becomes too great. I have seen this with elders that do not understand their role and they are thrust into a mediation role they were never trained in for. The phrase unity in the faith tells us where our oneness comes from. It isn't based on agreeing on side issues, as important as they may seem. Unity in our faith is our unity in Christ. He breaks down the walls and gives us the ministry of reconciliation.

EQUIP FOR THE KNOWLEDGE OF THE SON OF GOD

Why didn't I see this progression before? As we grow in unity and love for each other, we realize our need to learn how to be more intimate with Jesus. My wife is an equipper on how to have a closer relationship with God. In our journey, we have spent years in a traditional culture that never taught us how to encounter and hear the voice of God. The answer was always, "Pray more and read the Bible more." It was never, "what is God saying to you?"

WE MUST LEARN HOW TO BE INTIMATE WITH GOD

In Philippians 3:10 the Apostle Paul wrote, "And I continually long to know the wonders of Jesus more fully and to experience the overflowing power of his resurrection working in me. I will be one with him in his sufferings and I will be one with him in his death." (TPT) We all value this, but how often do we use language which explains that this as a primary function of equipping?

In the midst of a major shift in the Spirit in the mid 1990's, we learned the value of dreams, visions, encounters, and spending time in His presence. In the process our love and appreciation for the written word of God deepened. It is the Word and the Spirit working hand in hand to experience and grow in the knowledge of the Son of God.

In our church we took seriously ways to help each person hear the voice of God for themselves. We taught people how to spend time in His presence getting revelation and breakthrough. This is why a church that puts a high emphasis on worship creates a culture of encounters. "As we contemplate His glory we are transformed into His likeness." (2 Corinthians 3:18, NIV). These truths can be taught and imparted and make all the difference as we train and release people into their purpose.

"AND BE MATURE"

Verse 13 continues simply with, "And be mature..." For me it is another light that goes on. We need to equip what maturity looks like. When preaching on maturity I will often ask people if they are mature. You would be surprised how few hands go up. I've learned that it is because people don't often have a way to measure it.

CAN WE TELL PEOPLE THEY ARE IMMATURE?

I believe that most people would find telling them that they are immature as being offensive or judgmental. Why? We all need to grow and mature in different ways. Equipping involves this in its nature, we need to overcome immaturity and come into a place of strength. This is the call for equipping. We can find many people who say that they know their purpose, but don't know how to get there.

At the end of this chapter there is a maturity assessment tool. The goal isn't to show you how immature you are, but it is to inspire you to see areas where you can come into greater maturity.

CHAPTER 5 THE WORD AS OUR GUIDE

ATTAINING THE FULL MEASURE OF CHRIST

This last part of vs. 13 relates directly to this book. We need to equip people to know and pursue their destiny with all of their heart and strength. Your blueprint is designed by God and He has given this destiny to you. As an act of maturity, we must choose to want the "full measure." We are called, but it takes faith to believe God and His word instead of the world that tries to tell us who we are and who we are not.

DO YOU WANT THE FULL MEASURE?

This is not a rhetorical question. The Greek words here mean "to come to completion, to fulfill, filled up, and fulness." (Strong's Concordance) This is not just any ordinary measure; it is the fullness of Christ. It is what Jesus purposed when he gave us the Fivefold graces that reveal the blueprint for our individual destiny.

Declare out loud, "I want the full measure of Christ!" This is not only in vs. 13, but is stated in Ephesians 4:7, "as Christ apportioned it." (NIV). In my mind and heart, I picture myself like an athlete wanting to break the tape in a track race.

EQUIP FOR DESTINY

That is why it is so exciting to me, because in essence this is my Destiny Declaration. When ministering to people in various settings it seems as though I want their destiny more than they want it. This is a challenge for anyone that takes equipping seriously.

KEY QUALITIES FOR RELATIONAL IQ

Before we advance to the next step, I thought it was vital to follow up on this challenge to equip relationally. This is more for reflection and growth, exactly what we need to be aware of if our blueprint is going to become a reality.

If you are going to move forward with the blueprint of your destiny, it is time to look honestly at your relational skills of the past. This process will be difficult. In the following pages there are some questions that lead to a "RELATIONAL IQ" Assessment. To prepare for this, let's go over some of the basic areas that need to be evaluated. These questions are subjective, meaning that it is truth as you see it and experience it. There could easily be more areas, but these are the major areas I have seen leaders struggle with.

INTIMACY

There are many ways to grow closer and connected to people. The key to effective leadership is the ability to actually develop healthy and influential relationships. Intimacy is not only physical and emotional, but it can come through shared goals, working side by side, and supporting each other through the challenges we face together. Let's face it, many people do feel lonely even when surrounded by people.

So here are a few questions:
- Do you feel connected to people in a emotional sense?
- Do you share personal aspects of your life?
- Are you able to share how you are vulnerable?

Independence- For many people the need to do things

on our own is very strong. It is rare and difficult to ask others for help for them. Even when we do, we don't want to be an inconvenience or be a burden. In recent months God has been telling me that my unwillingness to ask for assistance is immature and unhealthy. He has shown me that asking for help can bring healthy interdependence and intimacy. Relying on others can build relationships. On the other hand, we might not trust others to respond to us in a healthy way. They may feel like we take advantage of them. When we truly believe that independence and doing it ourselves is better, we actually can hinder our growth as well as that of others.

- Do you generally let people give to you?
- Are you willing to ask for help when you need it?
- Do you prefer to work alone, or do you make an effort to include others?

HONORING

One of the most important qualities of a leader is to see the value in other people. When a person is so focused on their own gifts and abilities, there is a potential that they might function as a lone ranger. Honor means that we can put others before ourselves. I believe that the highest benefit of the Fivefold ministry is that you learn to see the strengths and graces of others. Instead of comparing ourselves or competing, when you honor you can see what others carry and respect it. People want to know that you appreciate who they are and what they carry. The beauty of the Fivefold is that the expression of the different graces can make our lives richer and bring the unity we desire. However, this only takes place when honor is paramount.

- Do you often try to see the value of others around you?
- Can you state the grace and gifts that others have and encourage them to develop in them more?
- Are you able to defer to others when responsibilities intersect?

PEACEMAKING

This does apply to being congenial, gracious, and patient with others. It is a facet of maturity when we can work with people despite differences and difficulties. However, a true peacemaker knows how to deal with conflict when it arises. Since many are brought up in homes where conflict is avoided, the fact that there is continuing conflict can be a sore point. The truth is, conflict is a part of life. It can be healthy, productive, and healing. On the other hand, it can be unhealthy, unproductive, and painful. I believe that a mature person learns how to bring redemption and restoration during conflict.

- When there is conflict, do you shut people out and refuse to engage?
- Do you become angry because others distort or distrust you?
- Are you able to bring resolution and peace to situations that have severe tension?

HONESTY

People want to know that your word means something. When we are honest about our feelings and thoughts, but we withhold important information, that is dishonest. Also, we need to make our "yes" a "yes," and our "no a no." The ability to confront and "carefront" is vital to establishing influence and building trust. If we are elusive and hard to pin down, it can appear as though we don't care that we are manipulating the situation. Our ability to tell the truth, even if it makes ourselves look bad helps build a culture where people can be real and vulnerable.

- When you say "yes I will", do people know that you will genuinely follow through with the promise?
- Do you let things build inside or are you able to communicate about difficult topics?
- Do you take responsibility when you let others down or fail to follow through?

COMPASSION

Those around us need to know that we care for them, even if we can't always relate to what they are going through. People have different needs, some want to be comforted and affirmed, while others want more feedback on how to improve. We need to remember that the people around us aren't there to serve us, in fact as we mature, we are there to serve them. When people sense our genuine concern for them, it motivates and validates them. If we are aloof or unaware of their needs it can lead to a feeling of being taken advantage of or used. Listening to the cues and people's hearts can go a long way.

- Are you able to stop and listen when necessary?
- Are you able to hear it when people say they are hurting without saying it directly?
- Do people around you feel loved by you, and do they express that?

FORBEARANCE

A mature person is not easily offended and quick to defend themselves. Patience with others means that we are not overly critical or judgmental. I have often joked, "Dead people don't get offended." It can take an intentional choice not to take offense or get riled up inside. This is what it means not to be "quick-tempered," a basic character quality for an elder. I marvel at people who can quickly see other people's side, and are eager to bridge. A defensive leader seems to "strike before being stricken." If you use other people's weakness against them, that is a form of control that can be very unhealthy. You always want people to feel comfortable around you.

- Would people describe you as a "safe" person?
- Are you quick to forgive people when they hurt you or let you down?
- Are you able to accept the weaknesses of others and respond graciously to others?

COVENTAL

I believe the strongest way to stay out of sin and deception is to honor the covenants that God has given us. Our first covenant and love are with God. Following we have covenants in marriage, family, friends, contractual, and informal relationships we make commitments to. For some people, their covenants are taken lightly compared to others. Covenants guide us on how to spend our energy, time, and resources. We will give to the relationships that have value to us, and when that changes it can be healthy or source of great pain. Loyalty is a great quality because people know they can trust you. Faithfulness is a great quality because people know they can count of you.

- Are you aware of your covenants when you make decisions in your life?
- Would people describe you as dependable and consistent?
- Do you ever secretly violate covenants in any way in your life?

THE MATURITY ASSESSMENT TOOL

In the maturity assessment tool, let's apply what we have learned in this chapter and in our reflections. As we prepare for our destiny, this chapter has sought to lovingly reveal hindrances to the building of our blueprint.

MATURITY ASSESSMENT TOOL

"Until we all reach unity in the faith and in the knowledge of the Son of God and become mature, attaining to the whole measure of the fullness of Christ." Ephesians 4:13

Read over each area and then circle one description, 1-5. The goal is to find areas for growth.

1. **Ability to receive God's Love**, Overcoming Self-hatred (Jer. 31:3, Mat. 3:17, SS 1:2)
    1. God loves me because He loves everyone. I'm not that special.
    2. I getting closer to Him, but I know there's a lot of walls.
    3. I can draw from his Presence sometimes.
    4. I feel his affection and love easily.

5. 5—SO MUCH LOVE! Wow, it's overwhelming!
2. **Overcoming Condemnation** (Rom. 8:1; Eph. 2:13)
   1. I punish myself emotionally when I make a mistake. Deep down, I know I'm a really bad person.
   2. I feel shame often, it's hard to overcome it.
   3. I feel bad when I blow it, but I'm able to recover with some time.
   4. I repent, and rely on the blood of Jesus for my righteousness.
   5. There's no broken relationship with God. I feel so loved when God corrects me.
3. **Refusing Rejection/Offense** (Rom. 12:14; Mat. 5:46)

   1. I treat people the way they treat me.
   2. I avoid people that aren't nice to me.
   3. It hurts deeply when people reject me. I forgive them but hold them at arm's length.
   4. I can see people's wounded hearts and understand why they keep me distant. I accept them where they're at.
   5. I lavish love on people that don't like me. It's exciting to see God work through me in their lives.
4. **Walking in Obedience** (Gen. 4:7; Jn. 14:15)
   1. I don't trust that God has my best interest in mind. He's a hard task-master.
   2. I pick and choose when I want to do what He says. I don't sense His direction in my life very well.
   3. I'm learning to trust that what I hear God say to me is

good and am seeing fruit from following Him.

4. I hear the Lord clearly and want to obey Him all the time.

5. I abide with the Lord continually. I can't imagine not doing everything He asks immediately, with joy.

5. **Understanding Alignment** (Eph. 4:11, Heb. 13:17)

   1. I will never trust another leader or make covenant with anyone again.

   2. Three strikes and you're out!

   3. I will do everything they ask, but not give my heart. I complain behind closed doors.

   4. I am learning to trust that God gives me the right leaders, and am forgiving, but can still be hurt easily.

   5. I know my leaders aren't perfect, but trust that God has put them into my life. I honor, love, serve and receive from them. I pray for them continually.

6. **Overcoming Misunderstanding/Anonymity** (2 Chr. 16:9)

   1. I'm always alone. No one will ever understand me and I resent them for it.

   2. I'm so sad that people don't want to partner with me or honor me. Lord, help me to forgive them.

   3. I'm learning to trust that God will reveal things to my loved ones at the right time. It makes me feel lonely, though.

   4. I know God is using this time to learn to lean on Him instead of others. I don't need other people's approval.

5. Praise God that He has entrusted a unique calling to me. I'm so privileged to be persecuted for righteousness' sake!

7. **Fruit of Faithfulness** (Is. 40:31; Gal. 6:9)

   1. This season is horrible! I'm getting out of here!
   2. This is so hard. Lord, help me to endure this misery.
   3. I want to glean everything I can from this season. Where are you, God?
   4. Help me to be strong, Lord. Use this situation for a good reason.
   5. Thank you for the strength to endure. I'm so grateful for the every day of life that you give me.

8. **Healing of Inner Wounds** (Is. 42:3; Jn. 10:11)

   1. I can't trust You, God. You don't care about me at all. I choose to close off my heart.
   2. Why is this happening again? I must be a really bad person.
   3. Ouch! God, please help me understand! How can I stop this from happening?
   4. Lord, I give you my heart. I believe You are good.
   5. You are the shepherd of my heart. I allow You to go to those deep unhealed places to bring a complete healing. Praise you God!

9. **Unanswered Prayer** (Mt. 25; Rev. 1:8)

   1. "What's the use of praying...You don't listen anyway!"
   2. I'll keep asking once in awhile. Maybe one of these days, You'll change my circumstance.

3. I think You care, but I don't understand why things don't change.

4. I trust that You are listening to me. I will keep asking and seeking until I find an answer.

5. I rule and reign with You in heavenly places. You have shared Your authority over everything. I know my Redeemer lives and I'm God's special child.

10. Accepting Transition (Eccl. 3; 1 Co. 6:20)

1. I feel completely lost. I have so much fear about the future.

2. Lord, why do You keep taking things away? I don't know who I am without those roles?

3. I'm not excited about change. I have finally found my place, but I'm willing to try to follow You!

4. I'm not sure where You're taking me, but I know that You are working all things for my good.

5. Wow, Lord, You must really trust me for an amazing promotion in the Spirit!

11. **Living in Community** (Jn. 13:34)

1. Nobody likes me. I'm on my own.

2. I think I'm right about most stuff. I enjoy being with people that agree with me and appreciate me.

3. I'm learning to "show up" emotionally with a healthy give and take, although it's still challenging for me to feel like I'm a vital part.

4. I reach out to others to validate them and make them feel a part. I know the importance of working together in the Kingdom.

5. I know who I'm called to work with and love others deeply and let them love me. I'm able to work through difficult issues with others to accomplish amazing things in the Kingdom together.

12. **Overcoming Fear of Man** (Acts 4:31)
    1. I stay in the background and try to be unnoticed.
    2. I'm willing to stand out if I feel really confident.
    3. I try really hard to be bold and risk, but then second-guess a lot.
    4. I'm growing confident in my identity in Christ and am willing to try most things I feel the Spirit leading me to do.
    5. Fear of man is not an issue. I can't wait for the next challenge.

13. **Living in Intimacy** (Jn 17:23; Eph. 4:15)
    1. I know people won't like me if they get to know me.
    2. I'll share a few things about myself if the person seems extra safe.
    3. I'm learning to be more open about my weaknesses and learning to listen and care more deeply about others.
    4. I have a keen sense about what level of transparency others can receive from me and I actively engage others to share their heart.
    5. I'm able to commit myself to covenant relationships that go to the deepest places with healing and unconditional love.

14. **The Gift of Generosity** (1 Tim. 6:18; Eph. 1:18)
    1. I feel very needy on many levels. I'm desperate for

others to give to me.

2. I'm learning that I'm a daughter/son of the King, but I don't feel it very much yet.

3. Some things are easy to share (finances, energy, time, etc), and others things are difficult.

4. I know that God multiplies the seed that I sow. I know He cares about my needs.

5. I've surrendered all I am and own to the Kingdom. I trust God completely to provide everything I need.

15. **Proper Pacing** (Matt. 11:29; Mk 8:25)

1. I work as hard as I can all the time. If I don't do it, it won't get done.

2. I try to take time off and rest, but there's so much to do.

3. I'm getting better at making boundaries and priorities, but I hate to disappoint people.

4. I take a regular day off every week and enjoy the Lord's Presence to sustain me, but it's hard to feel that inward peace continually.

5. I only do what I see the Father doing. His affirmation is enough for me.

16. **Joy in Suffering** (James 1:2, Rom. 5:3-5)

1. I hate my life. I want to die.

2. I can't believe I have to go through this.

3. I'm trying not to whine.

4. I trust you, God, to impart Your joy to me.

5. I'm privileged to share in the sufferings of Christ.

17. **Refusing Spiritual Pride** (Phil. 2:3, Eph. 4:2-3)
    1. I can't believe you can be so dumb.
    2. How long will you struggle like this?
    3. If you'd only listen to me, you're life would be better.
    4. I understand why you struggle, I'm learning to be patient with you.
    5. "No temptation is uncommon to man." I know I have struggled with the same heart issues. Praise God for His grace.

18. **Fivefold Focus** (Eph 4:7, 11-16)
    1. I don't know what my fivefold ministry is.
    2. I know my primary and secondary fivefold anointings and am growing in them.
    3. I am intentional and being mentored or part of a group to mature in my calling.
    4. I know my destiny and am leading a team with people with a similar call.
    5. I am raising others up and duplicating in my primary fivefold.

19. **Moving in the Supernatural** (Luke 9:1-2, Matthew 10:8)
    1. I don't even think about praying for the sick or casting out demons.
    2. I am not confident to do this, but believe others can.
    3. I bring others for healing or freedom to my pastor or spiritual leaders
    4. I pray regularly for the sick and release freedom when I can.

5. I am raising others in healing and deliverance ministry.

20. Hearing God's Voice (John 10:3-5, Eph 1:17-18)

1. I can't hear God's voice really.
2. I regularly hear what God is saying to me and it blesses me.
3. Occasionally I prophesy over others the love of God and words of encouragement.
4. Hearing God and prophesying are a way of life for me.
5. I am raising others up to hear God and move in prophesy

While this is not scientific (and subjective), total your score and write the total here: _____

1-20,   Now you have areas to focus

21-39, You are growing and need mentorship

40-59, You are overcoming and ready to lead

60-79, God has done a great work in you and you can duplicate

80-99, The Lord has healed you and released you into your purpose.

100, WOW!

TOOLS FOR GROWTH

- Declaration
- Journaling
- Prayer partners
- Accountability partners, deep friendships
- Soaking in God's Presence, Encounters
- Forgiving (especially parents and self)
- Impartation (even from heaven)
- Breaking off generational curses
- Seeking different faces of God
- Memorizing scripture.
- Decisions to let go of ungodly beliefs
- Thanksgiving
- Never give up, keep going
- Accountability in schedule
- Recognizing patterns of attack
- Lifestyle of inner healing
- Establishing a joy center
- Prophetic ministry (self-prophecy, collecting and contending with others' prophecies.)
- Inner healing with professionals (Sozo, Theophostics, Restoring the Foundations.)

This tool was written by Ann Tubbs, and modified by Mark Tubbs. Any feedback would be helpful as it is still in development.

CHAPTER 6

SEEING THROUGH THE EYES OF GOD AND OTHERS

STEP 4, DETERMINE THE VIEW

When reading a blueprint, the View refers to the three different perspectives that the drawing represents. The standard **Plan** view is from the top. As it relates to this application this is from God's point of view. He does have a perspective that we all want to know and cherish. The second view in a blueprint is the **Elevation**, which is the view from the front. In our analogy we must ask the question, "How do others see me?" The third view in a blueprint is called the **Sectional**. This focuses on areas where there is a connection and overlapping with other parts of the structure. As we evaluated in the last chapter, our lives intertwine with others in a variety of ways. Previously we considered our ability to relate to others, but in this chapter, we will seek to measure how our actions impact others.

GOD'S VIEW

To understand "God's View" we need to know Him better. To grow in our destiny and maturity, we achieve this by doing closer to God. He is our first love, and the first commandment joyfully tells us that our main goal is to love God with our entire being. He is where we go to find life and love. Our call and purpose revolve around God as our very source and foundation. How do we do this? We get to know Him and His goodness. In time we get to see things from a Godly point of view. This changes everything!

Wouldn't it be amazing if we could see everything from God's perspective? He is in fact our Creator. He knows everything about us and what our purpose is. Unfortunately, we didn't come out of the womb with a manual for our unique model. Even as a seminary graduate and pastor for 11 years, there really hasn't been any church or ministry to teach me how to hear God's voice. There was the subtle implication that God's written word was all we needed. There was the inference that He rarely spoke today to people like what we witness in the Bible. This is a form of secular humanism, that teaches that we shouldn't rely or depend on the supernatural. A result is that the ability to hear God became something that shouldn't be trusted or be considered accurate.

In 1995, after 11 years of full-time ministry, that all changed. I record the process and testimony of this in my book entitled, "The Five Fingers of God," but it is important to summarize here. Through the physical healing of a friend and the hunger of some of those around me, we experienced a breakthrough in how to hear God's voice clearly. I would never say we could hear perfectly, but we did begin to receive very specific and accurate words that changed all our lives. As I did learn to hear God's voice, one theme stood out as the priority. He wanted me to know how profoundly and deeply loved I am. It was as though that is all God wanted to talk to me about, and to this day, this is how He leads me as I start the day. I believe it is a daily choice to receive His love. Without that, it is difficult to come into our destiny or purpose. It flows out of His heart and passion for us. For this reason, my wife Ann and I have taught people how to encounter and hear God at a personal and corporate level all over the world. Without this ability to hear, we naturally try to rely on ourselves and our own wisdom without realizing it.

THE ROLE OF HEARING GOD'S VOICE

One of the primary attacks of the enemy is to somehow cause us to lose confidence in our ability to hear God's voice clearly. The purpose of hearing God's voice and the gifts of prophesy are to know God's love and to receive confirmation of our identity from Him. I have found that the Lord is eager to share His heart and to give revelation to His heart and will for us. One of my favorite verses is found in Ephesians 1:17, "I keep asking that the God of our Lord Jesus Christ, the glorious Father, may give you the Spirit of wisdom and revelation, so that you may know him better." (NIV). The essence of this verse is that we need both wisdom and revelation. Wisdom is common to us, but it has more to do with a sense of God's ways than is about being "smart." Revelation is about that which is hidden in our natural minds, and only that which is revealed by the Holy Spirit. Yet, the goal of both is the same, to "know Jesus better."

When I began to hear God's voice through the Holy Spirit,

His love filled my heart to the point of being overwhelmed. What a feeling, overflowing with love to the point I was going to burst. In time the Holy Spirit began to declare my destiny and purpose to me. God was the first to call me an apostle, but He told me to never seek the title and in due time it would come naturally and freely from others. It took nearly 10 years for that to become a reality, but the title wasn't His goal, it was the function of serving Him and the body of Christ. In time the Spirit brought great clarity as to what that was to look like. This process doesn't end either, I am still getting exciting revelations of new doors and spheres of influence that the Lord has prepared for me. Critics of the apostolic movement distort and discredit that apostles are for today. This is explained to detail in my book, RELATIONAL TRANSFORMATION

Sticking to my point here, it is crucial that you gain confidence in hearing God for yourself. This is how you can know what "God's View" is. It is important you compare yourself and how you hear (or don't hear) others. We all hear differently, in the same way that we all experience Him differently. If we are unable to hear for ourselves, it often causes uncertainty in our lives. Remember the primary goal isn't to hear, it is to "know him better."

Over the years the Spirit has told me things I was called to do that my natural mind didn't understand. I had to quiet my doubts, experience false humility, and fear of man's judgment I had to choose to believe and obey God more than my own understanding. In the context of community and covenant we can test what we hear. The greater things are the more important it is to respond with faith.

CHAPTER 6 | SEEING THROUGH THE EYES OF GOD AND OTHERS

For example, in September 2018 the Lord spoke to me and said, "It is the season to shift nations." He said it again to my spirit, "It is the time to shift nations." I wasn't totally getting it, so the Spirit spoke with greater fervor, "It is time for you to be a part of shifting nations." Of course, that was hard to know exactly what it means and what to do. It is both humbling and challenging. The Lord clarified and answered my prayer, "Listen to how people invite you to come to them." As he spoke this practical counsel, I did listen to the invitations and the changes in them. Before this word the invitations sounded something like this, "Please come and speak on the Fivefold", or "We would like you to come and teach on the apostolic and prophetic." I loved doing this and have done such meetings for over 20 years. Yet suddenly the invitations changed, "Please come and help us release the Father's heart in our nation," "Can you come and start a prophetic movement in our region?" and "We need you to come and raise up the Fivefold in our country." These are real examples and they exactly aligned with what God had told me about my call. He told me, "You are called not only to minister to leaders and churches, but to leaders of movements."

I share these words just as an example of what "God's view" may sound like. He wants to show you the steps and nature of your call. It comes over time as you are faithful with what He has given you. This only comes by fresh revelation and learning to see from His perspective the best you can. The reason I am writing this book and developing videos and other tools came out of such a directive word. The Spirit told me, "I want you to impact more people around the world in the next season than you ever have." Wow, what a challenge! I now have passion to duplicate myself through materials, but also through raising up sons and daughters in our ministry, Transformation of the nations (www.totn.org)

My goal is to raise up everyone into that which God has prepared for us. My heart is to help others grow into their full measure and purpose. What an honor, I get to help people come into their destiny and go to another level in their lives and ministry. Foundationally, it comes from believing I hear God and what I am told to do.

THE ELEVATION, SEEING THROUGH THE EYES OF OTHERS

As we learn to become more effective and proficient in our gifts, we can easily become too reliant on what we see with our own eyes. I believe that a key principle in coming into your destiny is learning to see from a different perspective. In a blueprint it helps to look at the Elevation, or to take the view from the front. In this example it is seeing through the eyes of others.

This is partly why God puts you into relationships and teams so that you can learn and see through the eyes of others. It doesn't mean that our way of looking at things is not important, but it is more like a puzzle and other people carry unique pieces that we don't have. We need to learn from how others perceive and experience us. This is the "Elevation" or view from the front.

A big part of my personal journey comes out of trips to Kenya, Africa. My first trip was in 1998, and I have been going there at least annually for most of the years since. It was out in the jungles and the "bush" where the Lord had me teach for hours to spiritually hungry people. It

CHAPTER 6 | SEEING THROUGH THE EYES OF GOD AND OTHERS

was during this season that the Fivefold teaching became defined and real for me. To God's glory, we met a small movement in Eastern Kenya, and from there the Lord established our apostolic ministry. As we taught all over the nation, we raised up sons and daughters through seminars, discipleship, and Bible school materials. This history is recorded at length in my previous two books.

After going to Kenya for over 15 years, we had established a network of over 1,000 churches with the help of our spiritual son, Simon Karisa. I can't say enough about the humble heart of this man and the ministry he has established all over the nation. The year was 2014, and it was time for a shift. It was time to commission Simon as the apostle over Kenya. He had been running it for some time, but in his mind and others, it was still Ann and I that were leading the mission. We realized it was time to genuinely demonstrate that we understood it was really Simon's responsibility to lead the way from now on. Yes, we were and are his overseers. Actually, we are his "Papa and Mama", but we needed to transfer the perception in Kenya. While preaching one day in 2014, I put Simon onto my shoulder and began to preach. I declared, "Simon is above me here in Kenya, I come to serve him. He is the one who is leading this movement, it is Kenyans ministering to Kenyans." The importance of that shift was how people saw Simon and how they saw me. From that day I got a new title, "Babu," which is Grandpa in Swahili.

It was that same year my apostle, Che Ahn, accompanied us to Kenya for the first time. When Che asked me to become the Executive Director of Harvest International Ministry, he affirmed by apostleship by commissioning me in August of 2006. Every year until this day, HIM has sown into Kenya and honored our work there. In fact, it is called, Harvest International Ministry Kenya. It is an amazing story, but after we commissioned Simon, the movement went from 1,000 churches to 3,000 in a matter of two to three years. Now, at the time of this writing, December 2023, there are nearly 7,200 churches!

What I am about to say here may be the most profound thing in this book. Sometimes your destiny is fulfilled by making others greater than you! You don't have to be the one who does it all, in fact, there are others waiting for your impartation. Jesus chose 12 to change the world. We must learn to see through other people's eyes and empower them.

A significant example of this took place on a trip to Kenya in a following year. We were in a van traveling as a team from the hotel in Bamburi to the coastal town of Mtwapa. On the way our van passed a prison gate as we had many times before. I had probably driven by that prison over 100 times or more over the previous 10 years. Suddenly a team member asked, "Is that a prison? Have you ever been in there?" The Spirit had been telling me that the key to break through was to see through the eyes of others. So now my mind was keen for these types of questions.

I responded to the young man and said, "No, we have never been in there. Would you like to take a team tomorrow?" He was excited and took a small team of five people with him the next day. When they got back to the hotel after a long day, I asked the man how it went. Brian replied, "We were able to prophesy over eight hundred of the inmates. Tomorrow we will go back to share with as many as we can. There are 2,000 inmates there!" It struck me to the core, and I realized I had never "seen" the prison. During that season the Lord showed me through others, female and male prostitutes, influential governmental and business leaders, and other groups of people. I learned to see myself and my ministry simply by asking people, "What do you see?"

Earlier I asked you, what is your passion and burden? Now in this section we are asking others, "What do you see in me and for my life?" When these questions are asked of others around you, it can bring breadth and width to your ministry and maturity. It could change your life!

AFFIRMATION AND ACCOUNTABILITY

Another reason we look through the eyes of others is to allow God to speak through them about ways we are strong and how we need to grow. We live in sub-cultures that are critical and have a way of tearing others down. Most of us don't struggle with getting too much affirmation. We need positive words regularly, and to hear how people are blessed and impacted by our efforts. There is much we won't know until we get to heaven and God shows us the fruit of our lives. So, when we get feedback that is positive, it can be very encouraging. Mature leaders ask others for their observations and input.

Next, we do need constructive criticism that helps us grow. My wife Ann has heard some of my core sermons on the Fivefold ministry and other topics. I really appreciate how she can step back after a sermon and give me feedback. Sometimes to my shock she will say, "That was the clearest and best communication of that ever." However, other times it is, "It went too long" or "Your main point wasn't clear enough." She is generally very positive, but I appreciate it when she gives specific and clear pointers on how to improve. I'm a better preacher and teacher because of her.

It can be vulnerable to ask people what they really think. Early I shared about asking people for help. This came out of the Lord ministering to me about this. He was challenging me to learn how to ask others for help to build relationships and trust. As a part of that process, I asked three people what it was like when I did or didn't ask for help. One person, Linda, is quite close to Ann and me. She has been a friend for over 28 years and also our treasurer at both our previous church and our current ministry. She knows us very well, and frankly our life is richer because of her. When I asked her about the times when I asked for help, she told me honestly, "Sometimes you are too matter of fact and not relational enough." She was right, and it helped me view how I ask her and others for help. This past Thanksgiving, she came over to our house and we baked together, and I learned how to make her mother's coffee cake. We may have done that anyway, but her honest feedback gave a vital reminder. My wife Ann has said essentially the same thing. She has told me when I get too busy or overworked, I become too cerebral and impersonal. It hurts her feelings. This kind of view, both affirming and correcting can be very helpful.

CHAPTER 6 | SEEING THROUGH THE EYES OF GOD AND OTHERS

SECTIONAL VIEW, WHERE WE INTERSECT WITH OTHERS

The next view in a blueprint is a "Sectional View." This is when it is important to see where there is an intersection or a hidden inner working that needs to be considered. In a building this may have to do with the order of putting in electrical wires or plumbing before completing the walls.

As we know there is more than meets the eye, but this takes consideration and awareness. When Jesus said in John 5:19, "I speak to you timeless truth. The Son is not able to do anything from himself or through my own initiative. I only do the works that I see the Father doing, for the Son does the same works as his Father." (TPT) Sometimes we hear what God is saying, but we also need to see what the Father is doing.

This to me is the section view, when God shows you aspects that are seen by revelation of circumstances, situations, timing, and will. It is the inner working in you, others, and in situations that we face. This relates to the fact that we don't fight people, or flesh and blood. We are in a spiritual battle, and we face obstacles as well as experiencing the wind of favor.

To come into your purpose and destiny, it is not only important to see through the eyes of God and others, but to see in a sense God's timing and how His hand moves.

Let me give an example. On many occasions I will go conduct a meeting and there are variables that are unseen and unclear. Such as example is when I went to a church in China that was held at a health club. When I arrived, I found fifty believers eager to worship and praise God. After singing I went up to minister, and I could sense that

God was wanting to use me to release a breakthrough. I wasn't sure what it was at first because the intensity of their hunger mixed with God's love brought me to tears. Then I asked a question wanting to know their experience, "Do you know how to hear God's voice?" They looked at me with blank faces and most did not raise their hand. So, I asked the Lord this question, "What are you doing?" Seems like a simple question, right? It isn't really, because we often get into worship and prayer patterns without knowing it.

It takes an intentional effort to get the Sectional view. It is a decision not to rely on what you know, because God has a way of infusing new wine and fresh bread into situations. The Lord gave me a specific word of knowledge, that is when you get a specific impression. He said, "There is a woman here is known as the main intercessor of this church. She has a great heart for me. She has deaf left ear and I am going to heal her today?" When I receive these kinds of words there is always a little twang of hesitation, what if I am wrong? The intersection here is complex, it involves me and the people. In a supernatural way, the faith of the people activates the hand of God, and He uses those willing to be a part of the "Sectional View."

I don't want to give the impression that these words are always that clear or easy. On the other hand, I have seen God move so powerfully through these words. It is exciting to be a part of a team that works together in these ways. The sectional view is when we learn to see and hear what God is doing, and then we can be a part of releasing it in obedience and faith. This is why we need prophetic teams as a part of the ministry, to help see what the Father is doing.

Fortunately, the word of knowledge was 100% accurate. There was a woman who was the intercession leader of the church, and she did have a deaf left ear from a childhood infection. As we prayed, I gave a word of how much God loved her and was so proud of her. Then I just prayed in faith, "Father, please open her deaf ear now in the name of Jesus." Immediately the woman looked up and smiled and said, "I can hear now in the left ear, loud and clear." What happened next surprised me. Virtually everyone came running toward me, there was not going to be a speaking sermon that day. As we prayed for the group to hear God, I shared biblical principles and practical tips on how to hear God. That day there were many healings, but the breakthrough was to hear His voice together. What a joy! The Sectional view is when it takes many parts, and as we partner and act together, we see what God is doing.

THE INNER LIFE

Perhaps the greatest difficulties are not from the external war, but from the raging battles within our own hearts and spirits. We are so complex that it is hard to always understand our own feelings, inhibitions, fears, and anxiety. Sometimes we need help from the Holy Spirit and others to comprehend our inner life. Over the years I have valued journaling, which is a question-and-answer time with the Lord where He shows me my heart and motivations. That coupled with reading the Bible, has helped me use the sword to "judge the intentions of my heart." The application of these words is revealed as I seek to interact and live them out with others. In other words, "God's View" is experienced personally, but the "Sectional

View" is when we apply and learn to see together and in relationships.

In Ephesians 4:12 there i a call to maturity. As leaders with a purpose, we need to be committed to this truth as a foundational principle. The reason is that the more we mature, the greater our effectiveness. We have examined maturity as it relates to behavior, but what is maturity as it relates to our inner life?

My wife would often to tell me that she needed "inner healing." She wasn't being critical of herself, Ann just wanted to be free of condemnation and feelings of inadequacy. These feelings were deeply rooted in her upbringing as well as experiences and self-talk over the years. I learned from her that it is a life pursuit of coming into "His likeness." As people who want to mature, we need to make inner healing a life pursuit. This comes from organic relationships, counseling, mentoring, healing ministry from others, and most often, in prayer and meditation on our own.

As an exercise my wife Ann, (I know she is one of my favorite topics), memorized the book of Galatians in The Passion translation. For two years it ministered and overtime it chipped away at self-condemnation, false guilt, and shame. After that season she wrote her devotional called, "**Freedom by Grace**." It is a mixture of devotions, questions, and encounters with the Lord. It is a tool for freedom from a viewpoint that comes from years of fruit of the Holy Spirit.

Here's the question, are you open to receiving inner healing? Are you aware of the issues that seem to underly the pain and hindrances you are facing? Have you sought the Lord and others to get another level of healing?

CHAPTER 7

"HOW TO MEASURE YOUR SPHERE OF AUTHORITY?

STEP 5: ESTABLISH THE SCALE

One of the most important aspects of a blueprint is the scale; what unit do you use to measure? This is easy when using feet or meters. However, in the spiritual realm there is often ambiguity due to the overlapping of ministries and lives. We usually don't think in terms of how to measure our sphere of authority. However, could you imagine a blueprint that did not set measurements? It would be impossible to build the end product.

In the same way, every believer should have an awareness of their spheres of authority. In this chapter we are going to examine an approach to doing this. It is something that the Lord showed me, and I hope it is as helpful to others as it has been for me.

As we read the New Testament Letter from the Apostle Paul to the Corinthians, there are apparent relational struggles and tensions between Paul and the Corinthian church. I have found this to be encouraging for me as a church leader when facing similar issues. It isn't easy to lead a church, and the Corinthian letters give insights into how relational issues existed in the early church. The Corinthians experienced division arguing over outside leaders, spiritual gifts, and how to discipline those in sin. Paul, had to defend himself and his ministry with them. Did he have authority or not? This is an important question we need to ask, because abuses of authority generally occur when a person goes outside of their true authority spheres.

Eloquently, Paul defended his role in II Corinthians 10:13, "But we are those who choose to limit our boasting to only the measure of the work to which God has appointed us—a measure that, by the way, has reached as far as you." (TPT)

Let's look at the key words and phrases in this text:
"Choose to limit"
"Sphere of work God has appointed us, a MEASURE"
"Sphere of activity that has reached as far as you"

The word for limit here is the Greek word, "*Amertos.*" According to Strong's Concordance it is beyond measure. In essence, something that goes past or outside a measurement. Paul is saying that we are not going to apply a measurement that doesn't apply or relate to you. In contrast, we will focus on the sphere that does apply to you. He is stating that we do have authority in this situation.

In the The Passion Translation, this is translated as the "measure of work..." In context, this is a specific sphere of service that applies directly to the relationship of Paul with the Corinthians. Paul also uses another word for measure that we discussed before, the Greek word "*Metron.*" This word for measure refers to that which is definitive, measurable, and fixed. In this passage it is describing a clear boundary to his sphere of influence or authority.

CHAPTER 7 | HOW TO MEASURE YOUR SPHERE OF AUTHORITY

The Greek adds another word to measure, that is "*Kanon*", which according to Strong's concordance is a "sphere of activity", the literal Greek can be a measuring rod or rule, the kind that a carpenter uses. Other synonyms are boundary, rule, and line. Wow, think in terms of this for your life! We all have a sphere assigned by God.

He further explains this with the phrase, "God has appointed us…" It is a distribution or apportionment by God to Paul on behalf of those he is called to serve. He had a specific assignment that includes the church of Corinth. Paul appealed to God's authority and role in making this specific sphere and assignment to him. In relation to limits or boundaries above, in this case is appropriate and proper. This is important for us too!

This now brings us to the primary question of establishing the scale in the blueprint of your life. What exactly is the sphere of authority and influence God has appointed for you? How do we even begin to measure this? I think the key is to look at the spheres, measured limits, boundaries, works, and activities. The next section covers an approach that the Spirit gave to me. It certainly is not the only way to measure, but I have found this approach to be helpful and definitive. This is exactly what a blueprint is supposed to do.

GOD'S BLUEPRINT OF SPHERES

I believe this language is what a blueprint accomplishes. A blueprint defines clearly where boundaries begin and end, and when applied as designed, there is no misinterpretation. In life and ministry, the boundaries are not always clearly defined. It appears to be much more fluid and flexible, because our vibrant lives are not usually measured in this way. However, perhaps from God's perspective these spheres are much clearer and there are boundaries.

Wow, this is talking about you. We all have specific spheres or realms of authority assigned to us by God. They have specific boundaries and relate to the power and influence we have. Don't you want to know what these are and what they look like?

My goal is to show you that you have this defined authority, and it can impact every area in your life. We do not want to be pretentious or self-promoting in this endeavor, but on the other hand our lack of defining these spheres can hinder us.

HOW TO DEFINE THESE SPHERES

In 2017 I bought a Ford Mustang convertible. I had been looking for a traditional sedan, but then I had a dream to purchase a blue convertible. Nothing really spiritual about it, but in the dream there was such a feeling of freedom and fun as I cruised down the road. In fact, that has been the result of it, and it has been great fun to own and drive.

When we first got it, we were following some friends on the freeway, and we started to get far behind them. All of a sudden my wife Ann said, "Mark, do you realize that you have a muscle car under your foot?" I hadn't changed my driving at all, I was thinking it was a Buick La Sabre that we owned previously. Suddenly I hit the gas pedal as hard as I could, and now we were flying down the highway.

CHAPTER 7 | HOW TO MEASURE YOUR SPHERE OF AUTHORITY

As we grow in the Spirit, the Lord increases and shifts the spheres we are assigned. We need to understand the scope of these realms, to understand the spheres, and the measure of authority that comes with each. In time, as these change, we can identify this on the grid of our blueprint. We can see the expansion of influence in responsibility and influence. Sometimes the Spirit expands these through obedience and His power.

FIVE SPHERES ASSIGNED BY GOD

I wish there was a formula or easy method to know these, but I am going to share with you five different spheres that help me understand the scope and measurement of the call upon my life.

These are:

- Personal
- Relational
- Titles
- Position
- Revelation

PERSONAL SPHERE

The Personal Sphere is just that, the immediate realm in which you function on a regular basis. This is characterized by your being created in the image of God and having the basic right and privilege to govern your body, mind, and Spirit. By the way no person has the authority to supersede this unless you submit or allow it to happen. This is a more complex topic, but we can either exercise wisdom and authority or feel subject to the whims of others, the culture and other influences.

In Mark 12:29 we are told by Jesus that the greatest commandment is to "Love the Lord your God with all your heart and with all your soul and with all your mind and with all your strength." (NIV) This is a foundational definition of the personal sphere of authority. The personal is the sphere of your inner life and all expression.

For the believer, we give all of what we are to Jesus. He is our Lord and we choose to yield to Him in every way possible. We don't need to go through every aspect of this, as it is the most common and basic sphere that we are aware of. It includes how we treat our body, what we focus on with our minds, and what we set our hearts upon in terms of value and focus. Practically, it includes the stewardship of our schedules, property, and emotions. In essence every aspect of our personal life applies here.

However, to the extent we oversee and give attention to each area is not the same for everyone. For example, the financial life of each person can vary greatly. Some people are careless and carefree regarding financial planning and conduct, while others may be very intentional in their financial lives. In fact, some people suffer greatly because they do not take the stewardship seriously. Let me ask you a question. Do you think most people exercise their authority over money to the fullest potential? Absolutely not! People are influenced by their upbringing, impulses, advertising, outside pressures, inadequacy, and poverty mindsets to name a few.

However, the Word of God says we are the head and not the tail. We are called to be prosperous. It is an authority issue. It comes down to how we govern the personal sphere of our finances.

It is not my goal here to discuss this personal sphere at length. That is a topic for another book. My intent is to address the topic of personal authority and responsibility as it relates to fulfilling our destiny. A proactive, intentional, and Spirit led life is the key to coming into our purpose according to the design of our loving God. He is the one that designed the blueprint for our lives! The goal of this book is for you to define and declare this blueprint.

RELATIONAL SPHERES

This begins with God, but extends to family, friends, and fellowships. It includes those we covenant with, work with, and interact with. This is where our authority overlaps with others, which relates to respecting and honoring others. It is the overlapping that makes the spheres of authority difficult to measure. Where does your authority begin, and where does another person's begin? A lot of people experience pain and disappointment because of the tug of war and confusion over personal spheres vs relational spheres.

God has a purpose for all of our relationships. The most important and immediate is family, but it also includes co-workers, neighbors, friends, and even enemies. Many books could be written to cover this sphere, but in this book, we are asking about spheres of authority and influence. We need to understand where we have responsibility in the long term. Some people come and go in our lives, and we can impact them as well. However, there are covenantal and consistent relationships that help us define our sphere and callings.

THE ROLE OF ALIGNMENT

This alignment sphere includes relationships and those we choose to give our hearts to. The term alignment is a very important one, because it has to do with those who you give license to speak into your life. These are the influencers that you recognize. The word alignment is both relational and functional. It describes how people respond and interact in their kingdom relationships. The word alignment comes from Ephesians 4:12. The Greek word *"Katartismos"* is usually translated, "to equip" in the NIV and ESV, and *perfecting* in the KJV. It is important to connect it with the primary concept in that the Fivefold leaders of Ephesians 4:11, which states, "to equip the saints for works of ministry." Notice there is a connection or cause and effect stated here. Leaders have the authority and responsibility to equip the saints. The goal of any leader should be to equip and raise up others into their gifts and calling.

The word "equipping" is a medical term that refers to the setting of a broken bone so that it heals properly. When a bone is broken, it must be aligned properly for it to heal correctly. Otherwise, it can grow too small, separate from the surrounding tissue, or bend in different directions. This often results in a need for corrective surgery where the bone needs to be broken again! This isn't a fun word at all. The picture of being broken like this isn't something that most people would find appealing. However, alignment is the process that God uses to hone all of us into the maturity and fullness that He has prepared for us. This verse is saying that if we are properly aligned, we will come into our destiny and purpose. If not, it will prevent us from being whom God called us to be!

What does this mean practically? It means that we are positioned in such a way that spiritual leaders can speak into our lives. There are those we entrust our hearts with and who will care for us and be able to speak into us with Godly wisdom and authority. These leaders have the responsibility to mold, guide, and impart what is necessary for each person to grow into their Fivefold and broader purpose. The word equip is about developing relationships where spiritual leaders can train and release us throughout development stages.

This does speak to the character and maturity of the leaders; that is their ability to duplicate and equip others. However, alignment infers that those who want to grow demonstrate an attitude of alignment. This implies that they desire and seek out mentors, spiritual parents, and Fivefold leaders to equip them. As a local church pastor for over 24 years, I often found that people think and operate independently from leaders. I used to joke that ministry was like "herding cats." Some of that could have been a lack of leadership on my part, but it also had to do with an overall view toward leadership that I described earlier. Leaders were sometimes viewed with doubt, suspicion, and distrust. How painful for everyone. It takes faith for leaders and followers alike to believe in one another. This is the core of what alignment is about. It takes faith to let God align us with leaders and communities.

For example, Ann and I have been building a relational network that is entirely based on the principle of alignment. It is called Transformation of the Nations. This network consists of only those that have chosen to align with us relationally and spiritually. We have other partners and friends of course, but we want to know who God has put in our lives for us to increase and bless. For us it increases our authority and influence, as well as the relationships to encourage and uplift. This sphere of influence is easy to measure and is based on confirming who the Spirit has aligned us with. In turn, we have aligned our hearts with them.

TITLES REVEAL SPHERES OF AUTHORITY

When someone mentions titles, it is often perceived in a negative light. This is due to the abuse and distrust of titles that have become a prominent viewpoint in our current culture. However, I believe that this has gone too far and robbed us of the value that titles can give. Titles, when utilized property, have amazing potential for giving a glimpse of the realms of influence that God has given to us.

For example, your greatest titles are based on your primary relationships, they are son or daughter of God, brother or sister, father or mother, husband or wife, and so on. These titles have functions and include realms of authority.

You are a child of God! That is your greatest title, and the understanding of sonship can be extremely meaningful. We are brothers and sisters in Christ and this is vital for a healthy viewpoint of the kingdom. These titles in the natural make a huge difference. We honor father and mother, natural siblings, and those we are connected to through blood, marriage, and family.

God chose to appoint titles to bring divine order. They are not about someone being more important than another person. That is carnal and unhealthy. These titles underscore roles, responsibilities, and connections. When it comes to titles in the body of Christ, they can have incredible value for confirming our purpose. This is especially true when we do not give the titles to ourselves, but they are given by other persons and organizations that have the authority to do so. These have great value in articulating and determining our spheres of influence.

I Corinthians 12:28 says, "And God has appointed in the church first of all apostles, second prophets, third teachers, then miracles, then gifts of healing, of helping, of guidance, and of different kinds of tongues." The Greek word for appoint here comes from a military rank or a specific order. It is not random or arbitrary. I have not had the privilege of serving in the military, but my understanding is that military titles are well defined. There is an order, and each role has a specific line of authority for reporting and responsibility. The same is true in life and in the kingdom of God. Titles have power and that is why the enemy opposes them.

In most places of work there are titles and they have stated authority. Examples include manager, supervisor, administrator, director, and president. These roles define a person's role and the facets of authority that are assigned to them. In fact, outside the church, lines of authority are often much clearer than in the church. That is why earlier I said that we have lost something in underplaying the importance of using titles.

One time I was leading a session on the importance of titles, and I asked the participants to list the titles in their life. A dear friend of ours, Beatriz, wrote down some of her titles, many of which no one knew in the small group she was a part of. She told us she was a City of Rolling Hills Council Member (she later was mayor), Deputy district attorney of Los Angeles, Board member of five organizations, a child of God, and "warrior princess" (a title of intimacy she got from the Lord). "Bea", as she goes by, had many spheres that God had opened for her and each title reflects unique spheres she has authority and responsibility. If you review the titles, they were given by others to establish her roles.

The same is true for you. Your personal titles are significant and when you look at them, it will give you great insight into the doors God has opened for you. Take a moment to write them down and then list by them the role you play as well as the ways God uses you in those realms. What are some of your titles? Write them here.

POSITIONAL SPHERES

The first three are foundational and it is best when evaluated in order. However, the next two are more difficult to define. They are intertwined and a great deal of insight can be discovered through them. That is why I spend more time on these two to explain and clarify what your assigned spheres of activity are.

POSITIONAL

The word positional is related to geography, proximity, and lanes of authority. The Miriam-Webster dictionary defines this word as "of, relating to, or fixed by position. It also utilizes all three previously discussed spheres, the personal, relational, and titles. We generally don't use this word in everyday speaking. However, in military terms, a positional attack is essential. Also, in a blueprint all aspects must be accurate and positional. This is the practical "where and how" these spheres are expressed. It has to do with spheres of authority, responsibility and influence that are created by where you live and interact with others. We have all heard the saying, "the right place at the right time." When we have a life of faith, we believe that God places us strategically and He has a will in where we live, work, play, minister, and function regularly.

GEOGRAPHY

Let's look at geography with this focus of influence. God is about land. He called Abraham out of his comfort to a land of abundance. The angel of the Lord declared to Joshua, "I have delivered Jericho into your hands." Another example is when Jesus wept over Jerusalem and timed his entry.

Where you live, work, where your church is located and represented is all "Positional." We need to examine these spheres that God has given to us by our location. I have an amazing story to accentuate this truth. In 2012 we lived in Los Angeles, and my wife and I felt led to move to Portland due to a family situation. I was on a trip in August to Taiwan and heard the Lord tell me we would be moving to Portland soon. When I arrived home, I shared with my wife what I thought I heard. She said, "Wow, I heard that too and the Lord said it will be by Thanksgiving."

We were going to Portland the next week to see our grown children there, and we decided to look for a home while on that trip. As I prayed, I heard the Lord and wrote it down, "Look for a place in Hillsboro that is within one mile of the Hillsboro airport."

Focused with this "word" from the Lord, we went house hunting with our real estate agent in the designated area. The date was September 1, 2012. After looking for a day and half we came to some unlisted properties about one half mile from the airport. It was a townhouse complex and they had balloons and fanfare to attract people to see the properties. We found a wonderful 3-bedroom townhouse that went right up to a forest area, and we loved it. However, when we got to the sales office we were surprised as we were informed, "The units aren't for sale yet. They CC&R's (HOA Conditions) have not been approved yet by the State of Oregon. The townhouses won't be available until January."

We had been told by the Lord we would move by Thanksgiving, so we prayed about it asking for direction. I heard clearly, "Declare and command you will sign on Oct. 3rd." Of course, I questioned the Lord as they were not available until January. He said it again, "Decree you will sign by October 3rd." When I told our real estate agent this she bluntly replied, "What is your backup plan?" To her dismay I replied, "We don't have one."

Every day for the next several weeks I boldly declared and commanded in Jesus name that we would sign on October 3rd, so that we could close by Thanksgiving. Three weeks into this I felt led to look up the State Department of Housing that approved HOA's for townhouses. I called the phone number in Salem and a woman answered. I simply asked, "Do you know who schedules the approval agenda for HOA's?" She calmly said, "I do." I then asked her about the specific address and what the status was. She replied, "It isn't on the docket yet." So I asked, "Can you fast track it and put in on the schedule?" Then she said, "I would be glad too." Just like that it was now being processed! I hadn't even been transferred on the phone call.

As I kept on declaring and commanding each day, I knew that I knew it would happen in time. Then on October 1st my real estate agent called and said, "It is amazing. The papers will be ready to sign on October 3rd!" Thank you, Lord. This is an example of God's specific positional assignment.

Little did I know that the townhouse would be a part of our lives in special ways until this day. God has a specific plan for us to be positioned right at that location. Let me share with you some of these purposes here.

Even though we had a church we had pastored in the area for 15 years, we now lived further away, and I thought it would be good to relate to numerous churches in the vicinity. One Saturday evening I asked the Lord, "Where should we go to church tomorrow." I heard the Spirit say, "River Church Hillsboro." I went online and googled what I heard. Immediately a church name popped up, "East River Church, Hillsboro", and it was less than a mile from our new townhouse.

We went to the church service the next day and I remembered the pastor from a gathering a few years before, but we really did not know one another. Ann and I met up after the service and we asked if we could take them to lunch. Carlos and Pam Flores were receptive, and we went to a restaurant later that week. As we met, we began to prophesy over them. The Flores had a strong discipleship church, and they were open to the Spirit, but we weren't sure how they felt about prophesy. Pam is very tender for the Lord and began to tear as we shared words of life and encouragement. Carlos has a gigantic faith and he too grabbed onto every word. Even though they were open, this brought the prophetic more on the forefront and they wanted this for their church.

So, they took the next step and invited us to meet with their elders and leaders to minister to them. We were being "vetted" so to speak. That is what good leaders do. One word stands out more than others. My wife Ann went to couple and began to speak over the woman, "The Lord says you will be a good mother." The couple cried out, "We said on the drive here, "If they mention anything about having a baby, we will know they are from God!"

The excitement grew as they confirmed the accuracy of the words. In turn, they invited us to speak at the church and do a "Hearing the Voice of God" conference. We have had the privilege of dong that several times, as well as speaking at their church for services, retreats, and conferences. However, more than that we have become great friends.

The Flores and East River Fellowship support us in tangible ways to this day and we are highly honored by them. We love them and we are part of the family. That church has ministered and been a great support to my brother and to our son as well. This is all from God's intentional positioning of us. In a word, positional.

It's also exciting about the townhouse. We lived there for 2 years before returning to Los Angeles, but then it became an income source for us. Then in the spring of 2021,

CHAPTER 7 | HOW TO MEASURE YOUR SPHERE OF AUTHORITY

my daughter Loraina and our son-in-law Glen purchased it from us! Later my son Marcus moved in with them from Seattle, uniting the whole family in the Portland area.

God wants to position you where He wants you to be. You can have a title, but not a position or a place to function in. There are ordained pastors that no longer have a congregation for example. Where the Lord leads you geographically and physically can lead to opportunities for the kingdom and for blessings.

Paul clearly states, "our sphere extends to you" because we presented the gospel. He is asserting this reality when he says this to the Corinthians. He was a pioneer to them, and Paul knew that this sphere was from God. It took boldness to declare this. Sometimes we can be shy about what God aligns. This isn't about control, but rather learning proper limits and boundaries. As spiritual leaders we need to learn these so we can honor other people and their spheres.

I believe that we need to ask the Lord where He wants us to be positioned. If we don't have a peace or clarity, we may need to ask where does He want me to be positioned? Your authority and influence may increase greatly if you are properly positioned. It can also decline or be ineffective if you are not where you are supposed to be. Certainly, the Lord can use you wherever you are. The truth is we may be exactly where we are called to be but are unaware of the significance or purpose of it. This is the time to evaluate it. Are you maximizing where God has placed you?

Before I met Dr. Che Ahn, I had my own church in Portland as well as a network of around 250 churches in Kenya. Shortly after we met, he declared that someday he was going to commission me as an apostle. He did that both in Portland at my church and in Pasadena at the "Global Summit" of Harvest International Ministry. Later in 2006 I became the Executive Director of HIM and moved to Los Angeles in 2009.

Relating to Che opened many nations for me to minister. Some of these include Korea, China, Russia, Japan, Aruba, The Netherlands, Philippines, Bulgaria, and Australia. It was positional. I went from the Senior Leader to under Che and others, but regardless my sphere of activity grew immensely. At first with my position and role as Executive Director, and later, HIM Missions Apostle until early 2023. I am still aligned with Che and my official title is "HIM Ambassador." I have the privilege of representing HIM around the world. In summary, don't underestimate God's assignments simply through your positional spheres. Take a moment and list what it means to be where you are geographically and the position(s) you hold.

REVELATIONAL SPHERES

This is where God confirms the authority, He has given you in the context of "revelation." It is important that we do not give ourselves titles and positions, but we need the church, organizations, and enterprises that we are associated with to give them. This doesn't mean God doesn't speak and reveal these spheres to us, it must be done in concert with the previous spheres of relational, titles given by others, and positional authority.

With that being said, we must have a clear understanding of the spheres God is opening to you and what this means as you are called to release and impart to others. It takes great faith to believe things that God often says. We see this with Jeremiah when God told him he was called to be a prophet to the nations. Jeremiah could not receive the revelation because it seemed too great to him. During our transition from a traditional church to a prophetic church I had many people say I had an apostolic anointing. After researching what an anointing was, I began to ask the Lord, "Are apostles really for today?" I heard him say, "Yes and you are called to be one. Never seek the title but seek the function." I took that very seriously. People who criticize our movement have no understanding. They think we equate ourselves to the New Testament apostles who were with Jesus. That is ridiculous, we just honor the value of what Jesus meant by the function of apostles, to disciple nations and bring transformation. I never asked for the title, and to this day do not ask anyone to call me one. I do not rebuff people who speak in faith and simply see it as a modern-day leader that raises up and equips leaders. My function is different than a pastor or teacher. I address this at length in my book "RELATIONAL TRANSFORMATION."

This may be a deviation here, but critics of the New Apostolic Movement (NAR) don't apply church history. They simply clump everyone together, including anyone who is prophetic, and many others who are "apostolic." The NAR is not a unified movement, it has many different streams that have similarities. Dr. Peter Wagner originated this term to identify certain traits of churches and mainly movements that were (and are) impacting the world in significant ways. These writers dismiss the Fivefold so casually and then anyone who believes in them. My embracing of the apostolic has created a desire in me to honor pastors, evangelists, and teachers. None of the Fivefold is greater than another, and in fact, everyone in the body has an amazing call and is anointed by God.

Revelation of the Fivefold has made me a much more sensitive, empowering, and loving leader. I don't use my title or position to promote myself, instead I utilize these as tools to empower and enrich others. You can call me friend, brother, or as some do, "Papa", but I have no need for you to call me "apostle," If you do however, I will know that you believe God is going to use my gifts and obedience to release breakthrough in your life.

EXAMPLES OF REVELATIONAL

A few pages back I shared that the Lord called me to be an apostle to the nations. It was in 1996 when the Spirit spoke this to me, but I wasn't commissioned for over 10 years later. It is not something I sought, or initiated.

During that decade of preparation, the Lord mentored me in the anointing. For example, in 2001 in Matsangoni, Kenya, I heard the Lord clearly. This is a small town on the coast of Kenya.

He said, "Do you want to see what an apostle looks like? I am going to show you today." This is briefly shared in my previous book, but I will tell it in greater depth here. We had been meeting with around 200 leaders for several days. We came in love and prophesied about God's love for them in very personal ways. The genuine prophetic always comes in love and builds people up. This group of people went by the denominational name, "Pentecostal One Faith," and were led by their founding Bishop, Joseph

CHAPTER 7 | HOW TO MEASURE YOUR SPHERE OF AUTHORITY

Mbeya. The denomination fell into a "religious spirit" which has rules and regulations that don't exist in Scripture. In part, the leaders take their experience and mandate that same aspect for their followers. For example, everyone in the movement had to be baptized three times taking literally to baptize in the name of the Father, Son, and Holy Spirit. If you were not baptized three times, your baptism was illegitimate and thus you were not truly saved. Other rules related to women wearing coverings, foods, and lifestyles also determined whether you were "saved" or "backslidden."

As I prayed for the biblical word to give, the Lord led me to 2 Corinthians 3:6 where it says, "The letter kills but the Spirit gives life." From there I was able to share with them that the rules and "letter" that they had added to Scripture were a burden and hindrance to them for freedom. The Scriptures are the standard for the believer, and everything we hear, including prophetic words, are subject to the written word. When we add to it, that is establishing rules that it does not contain, thus adding to people's burdens.

It is strange how critics of the apostolic and prophetic ignore Scriptures and criticize those who embrace it! For example, they reject the supernatural gifts of the Spirit and criticize those who believe in them with no biblical support. The "religious spirit" uses the Bible to limit and control the people. I Corinthians 3:17 says, "Where the Spirit of the Lord is, there is freedom."

The people of the Kenyan tribe were bound by the "letter of the law," and they desperately needed the life and freedom of the Spirit. Good news, that is what the apostolic does, it brings freedom from religious ideas and control. The Holy Spirit is not "unemployed", we don't need to try to convict anyone. We love them into wholeness and freedom.

REVELATION OF THE SWORD OF THE SPIRIT

The Lord gave me a sword of freedom to release to the body of Christ. This came by revelation in 1996 when the Spirit was training me about the weapons of warfare, that we have according to 2 Corinthians 10. For now, I just want to share how real the sword became to me. I knew in my heart that I could wield the sword. That is what led to my boldness and understanding of my sphere of authority. The basis was revelational. This is a way that God shows us how to function authority within in our spheres of influence.

Another example of this is when the Lord told me, "You can increase the prophetic wherever you go." At first, I was taken back and even in a place of denial. How could I be used in such a powerful way? The Lord had to show me, perhaps because I was stubborn and slow and receiving this word.

Here is what happened, I was leading a team in Kenya in 2000, and we went to a region just north of Nairobi. A group of around 500 leaders were gathered for a conference. The group we were working with was new, and we were sent there by a leader we trusted. We arrived late in the evening and the conference attendees waited several hours to greet and hear from us. Since it was such a late hour, we decided to build up faith in the room and spent an hour prophesying and ministering in healing. An important note is that the men and women sat on opposite sides, as this was common during that time in Kenyan churches. A specific man stood out to me, and the Spirit spoke to my spirit, "A man here has had three church splits in the last year and he is very discouraged." The Spirit said he was going to comfort him and bring healing to his heart. I shared this publicly and he responded with great emotion and gratefulness. A moment later a team member spoke a word of knowledge that someone had a deaf left ear, and that God would heal them. A woman came forward and as the team prayed her ear was opened immediately. We prayed for many of them giving prophetic words of encouragement and life.

The next day the team came back to teach and minister at the conference. When we arrived, we found the people were not in the meeting waiting for us. Instead, they were lingering and standing around drinking tea and talking. I asked them if there was going to be a conference meeting, but those we asked said they didn't really know what was going on, only that the leaders were in the guest house. We approached the house and as we entered there were around 25 men gathered. They told us there was a big disagreement among them. They were at a standstill. The problem is that the doctrine of the denomination was that prophecy had ended and was not for today. Wow that would have been nice to know before we arrived! So, I asked, "What are you arguing about? One man replied, "The man you prophesied over is the President of the denomination and what you said was accurate and true. Secondly, the woman with the healed deaf ear, that was his wife!"

The Spirit had gone straight to the heart of the leaders. How could they deny the prophetic words and healings from the night before? Suddenly one man looked at me and said, "You have one hour to prove prophesy is for today." I took the challenge and began to share out of I Corinthians 12 and then chapter 14 on the prophetic ministry and operation in the church. However, after fifteen minutes or so I realized that no one was changing their mind. In fact, those who were opposed to prophecy appeared more closed and angrier as they crossed their arms. Those who were open were now leaning forward and taking notes.

I asked the Lord what to do, He told me to look for the angriest person in the room. A man that stood 15 feet away looked like he was thinking, "I want to kill you!" Then the Spirit said, "This man's best friend of over 20 years betrayed him six months ago and he has become increasingly bitter. Minister to him and encourage him." Oh well, take the risk, right? Then I spoke the word to him and told him the Lord cared about his pain. Suddenly the man stood up, and pointed his finger across the room and declared, "It's true, and that man is right there." Quickly the accused man also stood, and he began to cry and shouted, "I am so sorry, I was wrong, please forgive me." The men raced to each other and embraced as they wept in each other's arms. The onlookers were so touched that they were weeping too.

At that time, another man said to me, "What about me, does God have anything for me?" As he asked a dozen hands went up and they began to ask, "What about me?" It felt like popcorn popping in me, God had me sharing words rapidly and with passion. The men began to stand up shouting, "This is God, everything this man is saying is true!" Then the leader said, "Please teach us how to hear God and prophesy."

That weekend they were eager and hungry, but what happened at the end changed my life too! They were learning to prophesy, and at the last meeting someone said they had a word for the whole group. He said, "There are two people who are called to go to Rwanda to minister. Two men responded quickly, and they called them forward. After praying they took an offering to send them out as missionaries. Wow, they went from denying that prophecy was for today to sending out missionaries in a weekend. Not that long after as I was praying the Lord asked me, "Do you believe me now? Wherever you are sent you can increase the prophetic anointing." This has become a life word for me and catapulted me around the world to release and increase the prophetic. As I have shared, God give us realms to impart in just like Paul mentioned in Romans 1:11.

REVELATION AS A WAY OF LIFE

Jesus declared in John 5:19, "The Son can do nothing by himself, he only does what He sees his father doing." This verse has become a lifeline, and I have learned to seek this as a lifestyle. It is easy to fall back on to tradition, opinions, and experience. However, God is eager to reveal and release specific guidance and words for us. The written word is the foundation, but there isn't a verse telling you which property to buy! The words can be very specific and easily tested. God wants to tell you what to release, what to impart, and what to shift in your region. The Spirit will lead us into all truth, but also give us clear words of knowledge and wisdom. The basic truth is that you must know how to get revelation. Yes, revelation relates to every sphere. In addition, revelation also determines, declares, and defines the boundaries. For example, Jesus revealed we have the authority to bind and loosen, to bless and curse, and to increase and decrease. I ask a lot of people, "What do you release?", and you would be surprised by the blank looks I get from people repeatedly. This is a challenge to get revelation about the sphere of authority He has assigned for you. These five ways to measure can be articulated and measured to some degree. It can be more specific. I believe the Spirit will lead you as you ask in faith.

CHAPTER 8

WHERE IS MY MINISTRY?

STEP 6: INSPECT THE GRID SYSTEM

If you have ever read a map with numbers along the bottom and letters on the side, this is a grid system. This way if you are looking for a location of interest, you can find it easily on the map when you know where to look. The same is true on a blueprint. The grid system is the perimeter of the blueprint, so if you want to locate a specific area of the building it is clear where the dimensions and information you need is found. In addition, the grid system identifies where positions are and where aspects intersect with one another.

Wouldn't that be amazing if we had such a map or blueprint for our lives? Therefore, we need to know where our ministry and calling are. In one sense, we understand that ministry is limited by our physical location, a building, or a nation. Yet that is changing with online ministry and social media. Every area of life is a part of our faith, worship, and relationship with God. Yet a part of the maturity process is to know where our ministry is. This can involve not only a physical location or region, but also a specific people group or segment in society. It can be informal or formally stated, but it is real influence that can be affirmed by others.

In my book, "RELATIONAL TRANSFORMATION", there is one chapter entitled, Five plus Seven equals Transformation. This is referring to the Fivefold Ministry, plus the Seven Mountains of Influence equals Transformation. In this chapter it is my goal how to discern this more practically and assist you in focusing on where to focus your ministry. In the last chapter we outlined the five different areas or "spheres" that help you measure the grid of your life. Now comes the hard part, where do you focus and how does your ministry express itself? The grid system in your life is where your spheres touch down into real places and situations.

WHERE DO YOU BELONG?

One of the most important foundations coming into your destiny is knowing whom to partner and align with. For some, this is obvious and that's wonderful. They have a vital community that believes in them and is cheering them on. However, there are others who say that they have a hard time finding leaders that know how to equip and release people into their giftings.

Many people go to a school of ministry or have read incredible books on how to go to another level, but soon they realize, where can I walk this out with others? Many church leaders don't fully embrace the Fivefold ministry. It isn't sufficient to go to classes and then have no community or path to apply it. This dilemma makes people ask, "Where do I belong?"

CELEBRATED NOT TOLERATED

In the United States we are experiencing a huge shift. We've gone from an emphasis of tolerance to the impatience of intolerance. There is division at deep levels caused by political and spiritual differences. I believe the church is called to be the safest place in the world. When it comes to differences, it is a choice to celebrate others and recognize how these make us stronger at a corporate level. As we mature into our purpose, we must recognize the callings and anointings in those around us to be complete. In every ministry the primary gifts of the key leaders are valued, but often other gifts and profiles are just tolerated. In a mature and well-balanced community, we learn to celebrate what others reflect and release.

ALIGNMENT

Earlier I spoke about alignment in terms of relational spheres. Yet, we also need to address alignment as it refers to those, we partner with in the grid system. These are the people that have relational authority and responsibility in your life. We cannot do it alone, and yet, who will carry our heart and believe in us? The key is not to give up on leaders and the design of God to integrate and empower us. Our isolation may be the major reason we have not come into our destiny. The role of the Fivefold, according to Ephesians 4:12 is to "equip the saints for works of service..." We have all heard this before, but the word "alignment" is relational and functional. It describes how people respond and interact in their Kingdom relationships. God aligns us with leaders and communities. This is a part of the grid system. You are not just floating around out there without accountability or firm covenants.

TRUST THE SPIRIT TO SHOW YOU

This is a difficult topic and challenge, but to know the grid we must ask the Holy Spirit. In my journey we floundered as Baptists and we lacked maturity. We needed an apostolic alignment, leaders to equip us and believe in us. Our denominational leaders didn't trust us and viewed pastors as dispensable. As a local church pastor and now an overseer, I often found that people think and operate independently from leaders. It takes faith for leaders and followers alike to believe in one another. This is the core of what alignment is about, it takes faith that God aligns us with leaders and communities. This must demonstrate itself with real and tangible relationships, not just in name. You can be in a denomination or a network, but it doesn't mean the relationships have any substance.

EVALUATE YOUR CURRENT ALIGNMENT

This is a difficult topic and challenge, but to know the grid we must ask the Holy Spirit for guidance. We evaluated our alignment with the Baptist family that we were a part of. By the way, we sought to have a relationship with the leaders, but it became apparent over time that they viewed leaders as transitory. That is, leaders came and went, but the long-term connection was not the goal. Some leaders like me just didn't fit in. The denominational leaders ignored the growth of the church and listened to the few that were opposing the changes. My voice wasn't important to them. This now relates to my grid as I am used to bring healing, unity, and reconciliation where there are church conflicts.

IN ALIGNMENT YOU HAVE ONE ANOTHER'S HEART

My goal isn't to encourage you to simply disconnect, but to be honest. Do you care about the heart of your leader? Do they care about your heart? If you are the leader, do you have their heart or do you rely on your role or title? These are tough questions to ask. The primary foundation comes down to trust and the opening and closing of our hearts. We must sense that there is a call to one another and that honoring the people that we align with is essential. Unfortunately, for many the ministry is not relational. It is based on roles and expectations.

RECOGNIZE AND TRUST THE LEADING OF THE SPIRIT

For 10 years I served the Lord as a pastor in a Baptist denomination. I have never regretted these roots. However, in 1995 a dramatic shift happened as I witnessed the healing of someone with cancer. This catapulted us into a journey of discovery of moving freely in the Spirit, hearing the voice of God, and the Fivefold ministry. This journey took place within the context of the church that we pastored, and while many celebrated these new expressions, some did not. In fact, a core of leaders reported me to the denomination and the leaders concluded that I should resign. The Lord taught me a lot during that season, and in many ways, this taught me about valuing relationships over my perception of ministry. As we sought to sort all of this out, we were led to go to Pasadena and visit the protracted meetings of Harvest Rock Church in Pasadena. We did not know at the time, but the Spirit was leading us to a "tribe" that would welcome and mentor us into a movement of freedom and power. While I was rejected by some leaders, the Spirit was faithful to lead me exactly to where I was supposed to be. No leader, church, or organization is perfect. We need to recognize what the Father is doing, and nothing is more critical than finding where and who the Lord wants to establish you.

BLUEPRINTS NEED DETAILED SPECIFICATIONS

A friend told me that when an architect prepares a blueprint, they do not always take into consideration the strength of the structural design. This analysis is done by the structural engineer. When we examine grid system, it shows us the complexity of the building.

I need to point out that a blueprint doesn't identify all the specifications, materials, and overlapping aspects by itself. For example, there can be plumbing drawings, HVAC plans, electrical details, and other complex aspects. The analogy is true for us in that we must think about the whole picture as it relates to our inner fortitude, privacy, and public life.

WHERE IS THE CHURCH IN THE BLUEPRINT?

As we examine the grid, I believe the church is the context where these specifications need to be addressed. One of the greatest areas we need to examine in our blueprint is the role of the church. In today's culture the church is sometimes raked over the coals. The diversity and disunity of the church doesn't really strengthen its message.

However, our perception does not replace the Word of God. The Bible has very strong declarations for the church.

CHAPTER 9
FROM DESIGN INTO DESTINY

STEP 7: THE FINISH SCHEDULE

While we are always a work in process, there can be a strategy for a timeline in our lives. We can set goals that match what we have defined as our purpose. In other words, we can start to build and implement the plans on the blueprint. Some of this happens naturally as the word and power of God are released into our lives. In addition, as we focus, we can be intentional and strategic.

BLUEPRINT TO BUILDING

The goal of any builder is not simply to have a blueprint. The blueprints are not the final goal, in fact, just the opposite. They are critical to start the process correctly, but the goal is to have a well-constructed structure. This book has been focused on bringing all the aspects together that help an individual discover their destiny.

WALKING THROUGH THE STEPS

In this chapter I provide an exercise or worksheet to apply the seven steps of reading a blueprint. In each case there will be an example, and the most effective way is to share my process and story. Then there will be a place for you to enter your information. With each section you can write your answers. At the end we will finalize this entire guide by guide process with a life destiny declaration.

STEP 1: READ THE TITLE BLOCK

In this section we have the name of the author and the project. God is the Author of you! What does that mean to you?

EXAMPLE:

It is such a joy to know that God created me intentionally and knew me in the womb. After I was formed, He set me apart, Mark Tubbs, for a specific purpose and destiny. I am writing this and the following to declare that all that I am, and will become, is based on God's will for me.

STEP 2: READ THE REVISION BLOCK, FOR CHANGES, CLARIFICATIONS, AND GROWTH.

This is the part of the blueprint that records and recognizes significant background factors impacting the blueprint.

Here, we are examining the basic components for your destiny.

In this chapter we have the following equation as a guideline.

FIVEFOLD + PASSION + BURDEN = DESTINY

a | Fivefold

Have you done the Fivefold Assessment Tool yet? It is found in chapter 3, or can be downloaded from www.marktubbs.com/fivefoldassessment

After you have done the assessment tool:

Primary Fivefold Anointing _____
Secondary Fivefold Anointing _____

Write out a statement that articulates the essence of what this reveals about your destiny.

b | Passion

The next part of the equation is to list six or more passions you have. (My example is below.)

1. I love to help others know their destiny and calling.
2. My desire is that everyone will come into maturity.
3. My focus is on assisting others to know how God has set them apart for a purpose and that this has been measured out in the Spirit in terms of function and spheres.
4. It is my hope that people will hear the voice of God for themselves to know His love and heart for them.
5. My call is to release freedom to the body of Christ around the world.
6. My hope is that church leaders will know how to equip the people to their fullness.

c | Burden

The next part of the equation is to list four or more burdens you have. (The difference from a passion is mostly that you feel the weight of something God has put on your heart.

CHAPTER 9 FROM DESIGN INTO DESTINY

It is often something that has to do when our passion isn't realized.)

1. My burden is that leaders will free themselves from religion and tradition and have the desire and ability to release others.
2. I feel hope that people will not carry shame, unforgiveness, and inadequacy. Instead, they will feel chosen and empowered to do what God has created them to do.
3. I long to see the church value the prophetic and to raise up the Fivefold ministry.
4. I yearn to see the glory of God in regions to bring transformation and breakthrough.

d | Destiny

Now it is time to bring this all together in a DESTINY Statement.

EXAMPLE: MY PERSONAL DESTINY

The Spirit of the Lord is upon me for a purpose! My apostolic and prophetic anointings give me insights into this. For me, being apostolic calls me to help others know their destiny and callings and to equip others to come into maturity. My focus is on assisting others to know how God has set them apart for a purpose and that this has been measured out in the Spirit in terms of function and spheres. With the prophetic gift as a support, it is my hope that people will hear the voice of God for themselves to know His love and heart for them. My call is to release freedom to the body of Christ around the world. My hope is that church leaders will know how to equip the people into their fullness. My burden is that leaders will be freed themselves from religion and tradition and have the desire and ability to release others. I want to be used to remove the sense of shame, unworthiness, and inadequacy that many struggle with. Instead teaching them to know they are chosen and empowered to do what God has created them to do. I long to see the church to value the prophetic and to raise up all the five-fold ministries. I yearn to see the glory of God in regions to bring transformation and breakthrough.

STEP 3: READ THE NOTES AND LEGENDS

In our blueprint, the notes and legends are found in the Word of God, Example of Jesus, and the role of the Five-fold to Equip the Saints.

a.) The Word of God, Life Verses

At this point it may be difficult to narrow down your life to a few verses. In this exercise we want to list four key verses that describe your calling and destiny. Pray about this as it will be another powerful tool to assist you in defining your destiny.

EXAMPLE:

Life Verse #1, 2 Corinthians 3:17, Now, the "Lord" *I'm referring* to is the Holy Spirit, and wherever he is Lord, there is freedom."

Life Verse #2, Ephesians 4:16, "For his "body" *has been formed in his image* and is closely joined together and constantly connected as one. And every member *has been given divine gifts* to contribute to the growth of all; and as *these gifts* operate effectively throughout the whole body, we are built up and made perfect in love."

Life Verse #3, Ephesians 1:17, "I pray that the Father of glory, the God of our Lord Jesus Christ, would impart to you the riches of the Spirit of wisdom and the Spirit of revelation to know him through your deepening intimacy with him."

Life Verse #4, Mat 28:19, "Now go *in my authority* and make disciples of all nations, baptizing them in the name of the Father, the Son, and the Holy Spirit."

b.) Three Stations of Jesus for His release.

1. Baptism, Encounter of Love
2. Temptation, Commitment to Listen to the Lord first and foremost.
3. Nazareth, Overcome the Expectations of others and walk in the Anointing.

To underscore the importance of this in our DESTINY DECLARATION, it is important to include this in the expression of who we are.

EXAMPLE: PERSONAL

My deepest motivation comes from knowing that God loves me with an unconditional and consistent passion. He has revealed and poured out His love into my heart. I have learn to receive and hear the voice of the Lord and I declare that Jesus is my Lord and I want to obey in all things. As I walk in the anointings and gifts, I commit to relying on the Father and not my own wisdom and strength. As I walk into my destiny the fear of man and expectations of others and culture will not hold me back!

c.) The role of Equipping includes the following five aspects.

These are basic principles as it relates to me fulfilling my destiny.

Write below each of these aspects what it means to you.

1. **Build up the Body of Christ (servanthood).** My call is to follow Christ and to build others up according to God's purpose for them.
2. **Reach unity in the faith (relationship training).** I value relationships and declare that my desire is to love people as my priority, I believe my covenant to my wife, family, and community are more than my ministry. I commit myself to a lifestyle of unity and peace.
3. **In the knowledge of the Son of God (intimacy).** I know that apart from Jesus that I can do nothing! He is the rock, and knowing and following Him is my greatest passion and burden. I long to experience His love in an intimate way.
4. **Become mature (character development).** I commit myself to be humble and gentle, to always be open to the conviction of the Holy Spirit, and to repent and to grow.
5. **Attain the Full Measure (destiny training!).** By the leading of the Spirit, I want to come into the full measure of Christ that has already released to me!

STEP 4: SEEING THROUGH THE EYES OF GOD AND OTHERS

A | Plan View, from God's perspective

How does God see you? To do this exercise it helps to believe you can hear God's voice. Part of this is simply asking by faith, Do this to the best of your ability.

What are some things God has told you about you?

EXAMPLE:

God has told me,,,

- I am an apostle sent by Him to bring transformation
- I am called to increase and uplift others
- I release freedom
- I am bold
- I can release the prophetic wherever I go
- I am sent by His Spirit to those bound by religion
- I am full of life and power

Now you go ahead, write down some…

B | View from others

What are some things others have told you about you? (Be positive!)

- I believe in them.
- I have a good sense of humor.
- I make things clear on how to know our purpose.
- I have the heart of a spiritual father.
- I challenge them in a gentle and inspiring way.
- I walk in my anointing with authority and boldness.

C | *Sectional, Intersection with Others, How We View Them*

What is your attitude when you "intersect" with others and how do you approach this in your life?

Write it as a part of your declaration.

EXAMPLE: PERSONAL

As I go to ministries and various nations, I go with an attitude to serve and honor others. It is my heart to be humble and not to act entitled in anyway. My call is to uplift others and to release and empower them into their calling in every way I can.

STEP 5: YOUR SPHERES OF AUTHORITY

Under each category, describe briefly what the sphere is and what it means as it relates to walking into your destiny.

1. Personal, this includes schedule, resources, body, mind, and emotions.

EXAMPLE: PERSONAL

My whole being and personal life is under the authority of Jesus Christ. I choose to love my God with all of my heart, mind, soul, and strength. All that I have and am belongs to the Lord and I choose to give it to Him.

2. Relational, this includes your immediate relationships and covenants God has given to you. It also includes those you are called to align and partner with in fulfilling your destiny.

EXAMPLE: PERSONAL

My marriage, family, and friendships are those that I

have chosen to making a priority. I don't underestimate the role that they have in my life, and it is important that they get the best of me and my energy. I am grateful that my wife Ann is my life partner in every area that God has assigned to us. I have chosen to align with Apostle's Che and Sue Ahn and the global network of Harvest International Ministry. I also chose to align with my Transformation of the Nations family and am honored that I can be an apostle and spiritual father. I am committed to my natural children and their children as well. I am grateful for my friendships and I seek to love them in pure in a sincere way.

3. Titles, titles have been given to you by others, and not by yourself? What do they mean to you?

EXAMPLE: PERSONAL

- Son of God, I am a child of God and He is my Father.
- Brother in Christ, this is my highest title in the kingdom. We are all equal in Christ and our functional titles do not make us better than others.
- Husband, I am loyal and faithful to my wife.
- Father, I am called to be humble, gentle, and generous in every way
- Apostle, I am released to equip the body of Christ and stir up transformation.
- Prophet, I have the purpose of helping others hear God and declaring His love.
- HIM Ambassador, I have the privilege to represent Harvest International as an apostolic global family.

- CEO/President of Transformation of the Nations, I lead a relational network that creates a strong sense of belonging and support.
- Loan Originator, I am a qualified and honest loan officer that helping people achieve their goals.
- Travel Agent, I assist in creating life changing events like retreats, cruises, and vacations.

4. Positional, where has God placed me and what does that mean?

EXAMPLE: PERSONAL

My residence is in Portland, Oregon, and I am called to live here to pour into my family and the region. This means to love the people and to network church leaders. My home is a retreat center for those seeking fellowship, rest, and renewal. In Kenya, I am a father to a movement of over 7000 churches. It is my call to be an apostle and father to them, giving oversight, finances, and vision to my spiritual sons and daughters and to those under their care. Globally, I am called to assist movements in many nations including, but not limited to: Bulgaria, India, Kenya, Korea, Netherlands, Philippines and Russia.

5. Revelational, what spheres of authority has the Spirit revealed to you?

EXAMPLE: PERSONAL

God led me to Kenya in 1998 and I have been taking teams for equipping and releasing God's love ever since.

- I am called to the "religious" to release freedom and joy in the Spirit.
- I release and increase the prophetic anointing as the

Lord leads me.

- I have a sword that goes to the foundations that cuts off curses and hindrances.
- I have been given strategies for finances to have financial freedom and abundance.
- I am called to help others walk into their destiny utilizing the Fivefold and other methods.

STEP 6: WHERE DO YOU BELONG?

In this step we recognize where we are celebrated and called to align with to be equipped.

One of the greatest challenges for us all is to identify the community and leaders that God has for us.

1. Where do you feel celebrated and honored?

EXAMPLE: PERSONAL

My tribe is called Transformation of the Nations, a relational network of forty ministries and some business leaders that align with us. Our role is to lead them by caring for them, providing events such as trips and retreats, and encouragement through contacting and connecting.

2. What leaders are you aligned with and speak into your life?

EXAMPLE: PERSONAL

My apostles are Dr. Che and Sue Ahn. They have welcomed us into the global family and given opportunity to grow and increase. In addition, Brian and Candice Simmons, Wesley and Stacey Campbell, and members of TOTN have provided great support, honest feedback, and accountability.

STEP 7: PUT IT ALL TOGETHER FOR A DESTINY DECLARAION

Now, it is time to piece this altogether to view the blueprint for your life. There are some details that may be redundant, or even missing from this enterprise. However, it is my goal to provide some way to articulate and map out your destiny.

The following is an example from my life what I call a "DESTINY DECLARATION." It can evolve and change. Yet, the basic components remain the same.

For this, you simply put all that you wrote into a larger statement. It will take some editing as there will be repeated items or overlapping ones. Try your best to compile it and see what the outcome is.

EXAMPLE: MY DESTINY DECLARATION

It is such a joy to know that God created me intentionally and knew me in the womb. After I was formed, He set me apart, Mark Tubbs, for a specific purpose and destiny. I am writing this and the following to declare that all that I am, and will become, is based on God's will for me.

The Spirit of the Lord is upon me for a purpose! My apostolic and prophetic anointings give me insights into this. For me, being apostolic calls me to help others know their destiny and callings and to equip others to come into maturity.

My focus is on assisting others to know how God has set them apart for a purpose and that this has been measured out in the Spirit in terms of function and spheres. With the prophetic gift as a support, it is my hope that people will hear the voice of God for themselves to know His love and heart for them. My call is to release freedom to the body

CHAPTER 9 FROM DESIGN INTO DESTINY

of Christ around the world. My hope is that church leaders will know how to equip the people into their fullness. My burden is that leaders will be freed from the burden of religion and traditions and have the desire and ability to release others.

I want to be used to remove the sense of shame, unworthiness, and inadequacy that many struggle with. Instead, I want to teach them to know they are chosen and empowered to do what God has created them to do. I long to see the church to value the prophetic and to raise up all the Fivefold ministries. I yearn to see the glory of God in regions to bring transformation and breakthrough.

These life verses are my inspiration, Life Verse #1, 2 Corinthians 3:17, Now, the "Lord" *I'm referring to* is the Holy Spirit, and wherever he is Lord, there is freedom." #2, Ephesians 4:16, "For his "body" *has been formed in his image* and is closely joined together and constantly connected as one. And every member *has been given divine gifts* to contribute to the growth of all; and as *these gifts* operate effectively throughout the whole body, we are built up and made perfect in love." #3,Ephesians 1:17, "I pray that the Father of glory, the God of our Lord Jesus Christ, would impart to you the riches of the Spirit of wisdom and the Spirit of revelation to know him through your deepening intimacy with him." #4, Mat 28:19, "Now go *in my authority* and make disciples of all nations, baptizing them in the name of the Father, the Son, and the Holy Spirit."

My deepest motivation comes from knowing that God loves me with an unconditional and consistent passion. He has revealed and poured out His love into my heart. I have learned to receive and hear the voice of the Lord and I declare that Jesus is my Lord and I want to obey in all things. As I walk in the anointings and gifts, I commit to relying on the Father and not my own wisdom and strength. As I walk into my destiny the fear of man and expectations of others and culture will not hold me back!

My call is to follow Christ and to build others up according to God's purpose for them. I value relationships and declare that my desire is to love people is my priority, I believe my covenant to my wife, family, and community is more than my ministry. I commit myself to a lifestyle of unity and peace. I know that apart from Jesus that I can do nothing! He is the rock, and knowing and following Him is my greatest passion and burden. I long to experience His love in an intimate way. I commit myself to be humble and gentle, and to always be open to the conviction of the Holy Spirit to repent and to grow. By the leading of the Spirit, I want to come into the full measure of Christ that has already released to me!

God has a perspective and view of me, and I choose to believe it. Some of the qualities He wants me to affirm are:

That I am an apostle sent by Him to bring transformation, I am called to increase and uplift others, I release freedom, I am bold, I can release the prophetic wherever I go, I am sent by His Spirit to those bound by religion, and I am full of life and power. For all these things God gets all the glory and praise.

Other people's comments and affirmations are important to me. These viewpoints have encouraged me and given me a glimpse of my purpose. Some of these are: I believe in them, I have a good sense of humor, I make things clear on how to know our purpose, I have the heart of a spiritual

CHAPTER 9 FROM DESIGN INTO DESTINY

father, I challenge them in a gentle and inspiring way, I walk in my anointing with authority and boldness. These words spoken in love and faith are related to my destiny and I receive them!

As I go to ministries and various nations, I go with an attitude to serve and honor others. It is my heart to be humble and not to act entitled in anyway. My call is to uplift others and to release and empower them into their calling in every way I can.

My whole being and personal life is under the authority of Jesus Christ. I choose to love my God with all my heart, mind, soul, and strength. All that I have and am belongs to the Lord and I choose to give it to Him.

My marriage, family, and friendships are those that I commit to making a priority. I don't underestimate the role that they have in my life, and it is important that they get the best of me and my energy. I am grateful that my wife Ann is my life partner in every area that God has assigned to us. I am committed to my natural children and their children as well. I am grateful for my friendships, and I seek to love them in pure in a sincere way.

The titles given to me by the Lord and others are an indication of the spheres of influence the Spirit has assigned to me. Some of these titles are:

A son of God, I am a child of God, and He is my Father. Brother in Christ, this is my highest title in the kingdom. We are all equal in Christ and our functional titles do not make us better than others. Husband, I am loyal and faithful to my wife. Father, I am called to be humble, gentle, and generous in every way. Apostle, I am released to equip the body of Christ and stir up transformation. Prophet, I have the purpose of helping others hear God and declaring His love. HIM Ambassador, I have the privilege to represent Harvest International as an apostolic global family. CEO/President of Transformation of the Nations, I lead a relational network that creates a strong sense of belonging and support. Loan Originator, I am a qualified and honest loan officer that helps people achieve their goals. All these titles help give clarity to my destiny, and I will seek to honor the realms of authority and responsibility that God has given to me with them.

My residence is in Portland, Oregon, and I am called to live here to pour myself into my family and the region. This means to love the people and to network church leaders. My home is a retreat center for those seeking fellowship, rest, and renewal. In Kenya, I am a father to a movement of over 7000 churches. It is my call to be an apostle and father to them, giving oversight, finances, and vision to my spiritual sons and daughters and to those under their care. Globally, I am called to assist movements in many nations including, but not limited to: Bulgaria, India, Kenya, Korea, Netherlands, Philippines, and Russia.

In the pursuit of my destiny God has given me the following revelations that to remind me of my destiny. God led me to Kenya in 1998 and I have been taking teams for equipping and releasing God's love ever since. I am called to the "religious" to release freedom and joy in the Spirit. I release and increase the prophetic anointing as the Lord leads me. I have a sword that goes to the foundations that cuts off curses and hindrances. I have been given strategies for finances to have financial freedom and abundance. I am called to help others walk into their destiny utilizing the

CHAPTER 9 FROM DESIGN INTO DESTINY

five-fold and other methods.

My tribe is called Transformation of the Nations, a relational network of forty ministries and some business leaders that align with us. Our role is to lead them by caring for them, providing events such as trips and retreats, and encouragement through contacting and connecting. My apostles are Dr. Che and Sue Ahn. They have welcomed us into the global family and given opportunity to grow and increase. In addition, Brian and Candice Simmons, Wesley and Stacey Campbell, and members of TOTN have provided great support, honest feedback, and accountability.

I choose to align with my apostles Dr. Che and Sue Ahn. They have welcomed us into the global family and given opportunity to grow and increase. In addition, Brian and Candice Simmons, Wesley and Stacey Campbell, and members of TOTN have provided great support, honest feedback, and accountability. I also chose to align with my Transformation of the Nations family and am honored that I can be an apostle and spiritual father.

To the best of my knowledge and understanding, I believe all these things to be a true reflection of my purposes and callings in Christ. On this day, I declare that my destiny is given to me by God, but all things it belongs to Him. I dedicate to walk into the fullness of all that has been expressed in this "DECLARATION OF DESTINY."

ADDITIONAL BOOKS AND RESOURCES

PUBLICATIONS BY MARK

blueprintforyourdestiny.com

amazon.com

transformationofthenations.com/books

ASSESSMENT TOOLS

blueprintforyourdestiny.com

MENTORING AND MISSION TRIPS

transformationofthenations.com

TO INVITE MARK TO TEACH AT A TRAINING EVENT, EMAIL

drmarktubbs@gmail.com

www.ingramcontent.com/pod-product-compliance
Lightning Source LLC
LaVergne TN
LVHW012023060526
838201LV00061B/4433